art / shop / eat
VENICE

Paul Blanchard

pp. 112-113

Museo della
Comunità Ebraica

CANNAREGIO

p. 124

pp. 88-89

Grand

CANNAREGIO

Stazione
F. S. Lucia

SANTA CROCE

Ca' Pesaro

Ca' d'Oro

Canal

p. 34

pp. 8-9

SAN POLO

pp. 50-51

Santa Maria
Gloriosa dei Frari

Canal

Scuola Grande
di San Rocco

Grand

Fondazione Q
Stam

SAN MARCO

Basilica

Ca' Rezzonico

Grand

Museo
Corre

Museo
Archeologico C

Bibliot
Marcia

DORSODURO

p. 149

Canal

Gallerie dell'
Accademia

Peggy Guggenheim
Collection

DORSODURO

Canale

della

Giudecca

2

Santissimo Redentore

GIUDECCA

Isola
di San Michele

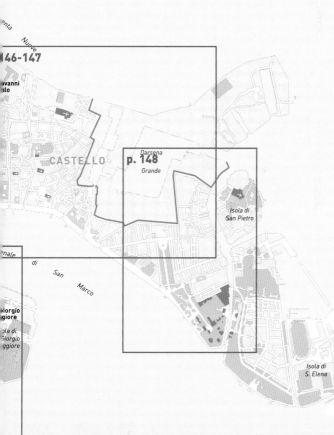

enta

Nuove

46-147

ovanni
olo

CASTELLO

Darsena **p. 148**
Grande

Isola di
San Pietro

nale

di
San
Marco

iorgio
ggiore

ola di:
Giorgio
ggiore

Isola di
S. Elena

San Marco

Dorsoduro

San Polo & Santa Croce

Cannaregio & around the lagoon

Castello, San Giorgio
& the Giudecca

entertainment

planning

art glossary

index

introduction

'Venice has been painted and described many thousands of times, and of all the cities in the world it is the easiest to visit without going there', wrote Henry James in *Portraits of Places*, in 1883. So familiar is the city that its image lives in our minds like a composite of a thousand picture postcards—and yet it is elusive, ineffable and changeable, a different city in the bright summer sun or the winter fog. 'The beauty of the architecture, the silver trails of water up between all that gorgeous colour and carving, the enchanting silence, the moonlight, the music, the gondolas—I mix it all up together, and maintain that nothing is like it', wrote Elizabeth Barrett Browning in a letter of 1851.

And nothing is like Venice. But to enjoy your wanderings to the fullest, it's helpful to know something about what prompted the Venetians to build such an extraordinary city, and to adorn it with so many artistic masterpieces. Getting around Venice without getting lost is also notoriously difficult; to explore the city serenely, therefore, requires a touch of advance preparation, a dose of patience and a sense of wonder.

art/shop/eat Venice leads you through the best and most important museums and churches of each of the districts, and gives you a pocket-sized course in Venetian art, including an art glossary. But there's more to a city than its halls of culture, and the book's shopping sections tell you where the best (and most authentic) local products can be found: from tiny boutiques of wearable glass art to elegant emporiums of Burano lace. And since the best way to get to know a place is to eat there, we've listed the best and best-loved restaurants and osterii.

A word of caution: restaurants and shops tend to be pricey, and accommodations might not provide the same value for money you've enjoyed in other Italian towns. But your author's advice is to roll with the punches. For it's as true now as it ever was that there is no place like Venezia.

SAN MARCO

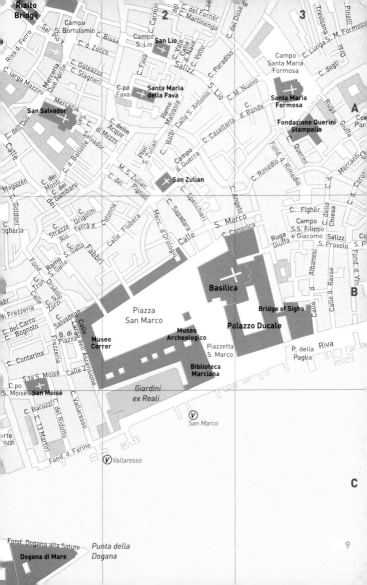

PIAZZA SAN MARCO

For more than a thousand years, the incomparable **Piazza San Marco** has been the symbol of Venice, the centre of its public life and its gateway to the world. From its origin as the garden of the nearby monastery of San Zaccaria, it has become today—through a long process of adaptation to the functional and symbolic needs of the Venetian Republic—an immense open space flanked on three sides by porticoed buildings, with St Mark's Basilica and its tall, free-standing campanile closing its east end. At all hours it is one of the world's most spectacular squares (Napoleon called it 'the finest drawing room in Europe'). It is most beautiful, however, in the subdued light of early morning and late afternoon, when the mosaics of the church come alive and the buildings take on a warm, golden glow. This is also the best time to avoid the crowds, which in high season can make sightseeing uncomfortable.

San Marco's horses and the Campanile

The adjacent **Piazzetta San Marco** was the principal gateway to the city and presented visitors who arrived by sea with the most impressive entryway in the world. No need for defensive walls here; the lagoon, too shallow for warships but too deep to wade, provided all the protection the city needed.

Standing at the waterfront, against the magnificent backdrop of the Isle of San Giorgio, are two Syrian granite columns erected in 1180. They are topped by Venice's two historic patrons: the 4th-C St Theodore, the city's first protector, who perches with his enigmatic crocodile, and St Mark, who displaced him in the 9th C, represented by a winged lion. (Public executions took place in the area between the columns.)

St Theodore and his crocodile

The piazzetta is bordered on the west by the **Libreria Sansoviniana**, a masterpiece of 16th-C Venetian architecture begun by Jacopo Sansovino, an 'outsider' from Tuscany who became Venice's most famous architect of the High Renaissance. Opposite the northwest corner of the basilica is the **Torre dell'Orologio**, built in 1496–99. The *orologio* itself is a handsome astronomical clock on top of which two bronze Moors (1497) strike the hours on a great bell. The event is worth waiting for—to see it you must step back at least to the centre of the square.

Beyond the Torre dell'Orologio extends the former residence of the procurators, the **Procuratie Vecchie.** The distinctive double portico was built in the 12th C and remodelled in the 16th C under the direction of Sansovino. On the opposite side of the square stretches its near twin, the **Procuratie Nuove**, begun in 1582 to a plan by Sansovino and completed in 1640 by Baldassarre Longhena. Napoleon made this building his royal palace and demolished the ancient church of San Geminiano to build the Neoclassical **Ala Napoleonica** (or Procuratie Nuovissime).

The Basilica

OPEN	The Basilica is open all day every day, but tourists are asked to visit the interior only 9.45 am–5 pm, Mon–Sat, and 2 pm–4 pm on Sun and holidays, in order not to disturb religious services. The campanile is open every day, 9 am–7 pm in summer and 9 am–4 pm in winter.
CHARGES	No charge for the Basilica, Pala d'Oro €1.50, Tesoro €1.50, Museo Marciano €3.00, Campanile €3.00
GUIDED VISITS	Available on request at 041 522 5205 or 041 520 9038
DISABLED ACCESS	From main entrance
SERVICES	Bookshop
TELEPHONE	Basilica 041 522 5697; Campanile 041 522 4064
WEB	www.progetti.proc.patriarcato.venezia.it
MAIN ENTRANCE	Piazza San Marco
GETTING THERE	Vaporetti 1, 52 or 82 to San Zaccaria stop

HIGHLIGHTS

Architecture and decoration, especially mosaics and inlaid floors	Exterior and interior
The Pala d'Oro altar	Interior, east end
Horses	Museo Marciano

The focal point of the square and the fulcrum of religious life in the city is the Basilica of San Marco, one of Europe's most idiosyncratic yet appealing churches. It was built in the 9th C to enshrine the relics of the Evangelist Mark, which were stolen from Alexandria, Egypt, in 828. The basilica's dramatic Eastern appreareance has remained essentially the same despite alterations in the 11th, 14th and 16th centuries. Its design was inspired by the (no longer extant) 6th-C church of the Holy Apostles in Constantinople. Built in the form of a Greek cross, with a large central dome and smaller domes over the aisles and transepts, it has been embellished over the centuries with marbles, mosaics and decorations, combining Romanesque, Byzantine and Gothic influences.

The interior of the basilica

EXTERIOR

The famous façade has five sets of arches and five doorways separated by columns with capitals of Eastern inspiration that date from the 12th and 13th centuries. The fanciful upper arches, with their imaginative Gothic detailing, were added in the 14th and 15th centuries. Dominating the centre balcony are copies of the gilded copper (not bronze, as commonly thought) horses brought in 1204 from Constantinople and now in the basilica museum.

The richness of the façade is a product of the architecture and the glorious mosaics that adorn it. The oldest, on the far left, is a 13th-C work known as the *Translation of the Body of St Mark* [1]. It suggests that the basilica looked then much as it does today

The carvings that decorate the **central doorway [2]** date from the middle of the 13th C and are among the most important examples of Romanesque sculpture in Italy. Those on the main outer arch feature Venetian trades, such as boatbuilding and fishing on the underside, with Christ and the Prophets on the outer face. The next arch shows the Zodiac on the underside and Virtues on the outer face. The smallest arch illustrates the earth, the ocean and animals, and scenes of daily life from youth to old age.

Walk to the right, toward the south flank of the basilica, and on the corner you'll see the wonderful 4th-C figures known as the **Tetrarchs [3]**. They are commonly believed to represent Diocletian and his three fellow co-rulers, but they probably depict the four sons of Constantine the Great. They are carved in hard Egyptian prophyry, which imparts a rough-hewn look as well as a rich and distinctive red colour. Beside them, the door to the basilica is flanked by two columns seized during the sack of Constantinople (see box below) in 1204, thought to have been made at the beginning of the 6th C.

The walls, vaults and domes of the narthex, or vestibule of the church, are covered with Old Testament stories in extraordinary gold-ground mosaics of Veneto-Byzantine workmanship. Particularly interesting are the 13th-C *Stories of Genesis* in the dome above the bronze Porta di San Clemente (cast in Constantinople in the 11th C) and the 11th- and 12th-C figures of the Evangelists in the bay in front of the main door. The marble mosaic pavement—one of the finest such floors anywhere in the world—also from the 11th and 12th centuries.

The Fourth Crusade and the Sack of Constantinople

Many of the treasures of Venice, like the beautiful Horses of San Marco, came originally from Constantinople. In 1202 Pope Innocent II launched the Fourth Crusade to capture Jerusalem, primarily to distract France and England's attention from their ongoing war. The Venetians entered as business partners, hired to ship the armies to Palestine for a hefty fee and half the booty. Venice had long had a grudge against Constantinople, mostly based on trade and disputes involving territory in Dalmatia. When the Crusaders became late with payments Venice asked that plans be changed and military might be brought against

Constantinople. This fitted in with the political agendas of the other participants and a course was set to take the great jewel of the East.

In the summer of 1203, the Venetians, led by Doge Enrico Dandolo, then over 80 years old, broke through the massive chain that hung across the Golden Horn to protect the Byzantine fleet. Soon political squabbling had the city in flames and in spring 1204 the Crusaders decided to carve up the city for themselves. The Venetians, who were crucial to the success of the encounter, were to get three-quarters of the plunder and a huge amount of territory. The richest city in Christendom was reduced to a smoking ruin, with countless treasures destroyed and much of the rest sent back to Venice and elsewhere in Europe. The 'Latin Empire of Constantinople' lasted another 37 years. You can read the whole complicated history in *The Fourth Crusade and the Sack of Constantinople* by Jonathan Phillips (Jonathan Cape); the sack of Constantinople itself is brilliantly described in *Baudolino* (Harcourt), Umberto Eco's fictional account.

INTERIOR

The sumptuous interior is an epitome of Byzantine decorative craftsmanship. The 12th-C floor, a beautiful medley of marble and porphyry beasts and birds, is fully uncovered only in July and Aug. At high tide, the floor shimmers under the water like a coral reef. (The ripple effect is due to the settling of the building over the centuries.)

All around the immense chandelier that hangs at the centre of the nave, the walls and ceilings are covered with mosaics. Most are by Byzantine and Venetian artists of the 12th and 13th centuries, though some—recognizable by their greater naturalism—were done over in the 16th and 17th centuries to designs by Titian, Tintoretto, Veronese and other Venetian painters. Along the upper walls is the matroneum: a gallery for women in the Greek Orthodox rite, here also an ingenious device for masking the buttresses that support the five great domes. The walls are lined with marble below and mosaics above and all is illuminated by the delicate lighting of the small windows.

The dome over the nave bears a representation of the **Pentecost [4]**; the dome over the south transept shows **Sts Leonard, Blaise, Clement and Nicolas [5]**. The **Dome of the Ascension [6]** surmounts the crossing, above the little relief of the *Madonna of the Kiss [7]*, worn away by the lips of the devout.

The two striking pulpits in exquisite polychrome marbles dominate the entrance to the **Sanctuary [8]**: the Epistle and the Gospel were read from that on the left, while the one on the right was used for displaying relics on feast days and also for newly elected doges to show themselves to the people.

The **high altar [9]**, which rises over the body of St Mark, is supported by four alabaster columns with New Testament scenes; it is still unclear whether these are Byzantine works of the 5th C or Venetian works of the mid-13th C. Behind the altar is the **Pala d'Oro**, a breathtakingly elaborate gold and enamel altarpiece encrusted with gems, made by Byzantine and Venetian goldsmiths

San Marco's marble and porphyry floor

between the 10th and 14th centuries and one of Venice's greatest treasures. Among the precious stones that adorn the work are emeralds, rubies, amethysts, sapphires, topaz and pearls. In the apse are an altar with six tall columns and a gilt tabernacle by Jacopo Sansovino. The bronze door of the sacristy is Sansovino's last work (1546–69). It bears the portraits of Titian, Aretino and the artist himself (Titian top left with Sansovino below, and Aretino top right). Beneath the sanctuary are the

BASILICA SAN MARCO

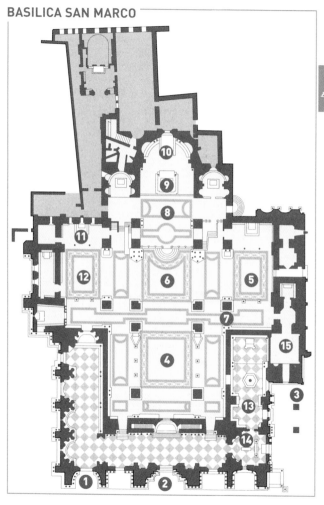

beautiful crypt and the little 15th-C church of San Teodoro, with an *Adoration of the Child* painted by Tiepolo in 1732.

As is customary in Byzantine iconography, **Christ Pantocrator** (The All-Powerful—a work dated 1506) **[10]** is enthroned in the **Dome at the East End** with the four protectors of Venice, Saints Nicholas, Peter, Mark and Hermagorus, below him.

The 12th-C Byzantine icon of the **Madonna Nicopeia** (Bringer of Victory) **[11]**, set in a magnificent enamel frame, gives its name the first chapel in the north transept. This is the most venerated image in the basilica, and considered the protectress of Venice. It was traditionally carried into battle by the Byzantine emperors before it was 'captured' in Constantinople in 1204 (see box on p. 14). Placed in the basilica in 1234, it has been removed only once, in 1968, when a radical cleaning revealed the glittering, enamel-like colours of the original, restoring life to a primitive image that exudes all the mysterious fascination of the Orient but is, at the same time, intensely human.

The dome over the north transept has pictures from the **Life of St John the Evangelist [12]**.

From the south aisle you enter the **Baptistery** (1343–54) **[13]**, created by closing off a portion of the vestibule. Here, by a baptismal font designed by Jacopo Sansovino (1545), are the tombs of several doges—including that of Andrea Dandolo, a famous man of letters and a friend of Petrarch, who commissioned the 14th-C mosaics of the *Life of St John the Baptist* and the *Early Life of Christ*. The baptistery altar incorporates a granite slab on which Christ is said to have rested; it was brought from Tyre in the 13th C and bears traces of an ancient inscription. Some years ago the slab was lifted and traces were found underneath of a rectangular font for total immersion, which is believed to have been part of the original 9th-C church. A door at the west end of the baptistery takes you to the burial **chapel of Cardinal Giovanni Battista Zen** (d. 1501) **[14]**. Here is a bronze statue of the Madonna, called the *Madonna of the Shoe*, by Antonio Lombardo. According to the story, a poor man wanted to offer something to the Madonna, but had only a shoe; when he offered it, however, it promptly turned to gold. The chapel also has a fine doorway and late 13th-C vault mosaics, as well as two Romanesque red marble lions that are thought to have once stood outside the basilica.

The **Treasury of San Marco [15]** contains a remarkable ensemble of religious art—a wide variety of liturgical objects, many of which were brought back from Constantinople in 1204.

Amongst the treasures on show is a small marble chair, held in previous centuries to be a throne used by St Mark in Alexandria. In fact it was made in Egypt, probably in the early 7th C, but later decorated by Venetian craftsmen. Many of the treasury's most precious possessions were melted down in 1797 on the fall of the Republic. Those that remain include an Islamic rock-crystal ewer and the so-called 'Crown of Leo VI', made in Constantinople between 886 and 912. The thick-walled room that holds the treasury was probably a 9th-C tower belonging to the Palazzo Ducale next door.

A staircase to the right of the main door leads to the upper floor of the basilica. The collection displayed here includes illuminated manuscripts, fragments of mosaics from the basilica, paintings, tapestries and antique Persian silk-pile carpets. Here, too, are the splendid copper *Horses* brought to Venice from Constantinople at the time of the Fourth Crusade in 1204, now restored to reveal their original gilding. The horses, thought to be 2nd-C Roman works that probably adorned Constantinople's Hippodrome, were on the basilica's façade by the mid-13th C. The horses were looted a second time by Napoleon, who swept them off (along with 506 paintings) to Paris for display on the Arc du Carousel. Other exhibits include the cover for the Pala d'Oro, painted in 1345 by Paolo Veneziano, and vestments adorned with delicate Venetian lace. It is worth coming up for the fine view of the piazza from the loggia.

THE CAMPANILE

Opposite the southwest corner of the basilica rises the campanile, erected in the 12th C, altered in 1511 and completely rebuilt after falling—fortunately without claiming lives—on the morning of 14 July 1902 (contemporary accounts tell that a crack appeared on 7 July and spread frighteningly upwards, spewing dust, until the whole tower collapsed on itself).

At the bottom is the elegant marble Loggetta (1537–49), with its ornate pink and white façade and, inside, a terracotta *Madonna and Child*, all by Jacopo Sansovino. Initially a meeting place of the Venetian patricians, the Loggetta later housed the honour guard when the Great Council was in session. A lift ascends the nearly 100 m to the top of the campanile. Galileo is said to have demonstrated his telescope from the tower; Goethe enthused over the view of the town, the lagoon and the sea. On a clear day you can see the Alps.

The Palazzo Ducale

OPEN	The Palazzo is open 9 am–7 pm every day between April and Oct and 9 am–5 pm between Nov and March. Last admission is 1 hour before closing; a single ticket gives admission to the Palazzo as well as the Biblioteca Nazionale Marciana, Museo Archeologico Nazionale and Museo Correr.
CLOSED	1/1, 25/12
CHARGES	Regular admission €11; children under 15 €3.00; students 15-29 and EU seniors over 65 €5.50. Reduced admission available with Venice Card
GUIDED VISITS	Audio guides available; live guide available on request at 041 520 9038.
DISABLED ACCESS	Yes (ask at Reception)
SERVICES	Bookshop, café
TELEPHONE	041 240 5211
WEB	www.museiciviciveneziani.it
MAIN ENTRANCE	Piazzetta San Marco, on the waterfront
GETTING THERE	Vaporetti 1, 52 or 82 to San Zaccaria stop

HIGHLIGHTS

Façade and the Porta della Carta **Courtyard and the Scala dei Giganti,** or 'Staircase of the Giants'	Exterior
Titian, *Doge Antonio Grimani Kneeling Before the Faith*	Sala delle Quattro Porte
Tintoretto, *Vulcan's Forge*, *Mercury and the Graces*, *Bacchus and Ariadne*, *Minerva and Mars* Veronese, *Rape of Europa*	Sala dell'Anticollegio
Architecture by Antonio Palladio, paintings by Tintoretto and Veronese	Sala del Collegio
Tintoretto and assistants, *Paradise*	Sala del Maggior Consiglio

The Palazzo Ducale, the residence of the doge and the seat of the highest council of the Venetian Republic, extends from the basilica to the water. Although there has been a palace on this site since the 9th C, its present appearance is the product of a late Gothic reconstruction (c. 1340–1420). Today it is a sturdy and enduring symbol of the glory and splendour of Venice at its height, to be enjoyed for the delicacy of its decorated surface as it picks up the reflections of light from the water of the lagoon.

EXTERIOR

With its vast walls of white Istrian limestone and pink Verona marble, fine porticoes, delicate loggia, magnificent balconies and crenellated roof, it is by far the highest expression of Venetian Gothic architecture.

The palace is joined to San Marco by a splendid, graceful gateway, the **Porta della Carta** (1438), with a powerful carving of St Mark's lion. The 'Paper Door'—possibly so called because placards displayed here once decreed the Republic's ordinances—is a masterpiece of Venetian Gothic architecture and sculpture, executed in 1438–42 by Giovanni and Bartolomeo Bon and their assistants. Its theme is a celebration of *Justice* (personified in the figure enthroned at the top with sword and scales) as the highest principle of government, accompanied by *Temperance*, *Fortitude*, *Prudence* and *Charity*. Doge Francesco Foscari, who commissioned the work, is shown kneeling before the lion of St Mark in the lower part.

Along the façade are superb medieval carvings (as well as some good 19th-C copies) representing the months, animals and foliage on the 36 capitals of the lower colonnade. At each corner of the palace's west wall, on the first and second levels, are 14th-C marble reliefs of moral exemplars: nearest the basilica is the *Judgement of Solomon* with the Archangel Gabriel standing above, while facing the lagoon are *Adam and Eve* (with a strategically placed branch of the Tree) under the Archangel Michael. The southeast corner shows a particularly evocative *Drunkenness of Noah* beneath the Archangel Raphael.

The magnificent **courtyard** is perhaps the finest part of the palace interior. Here the uniformity of the patterned façade is contrasted by a medley of styles united only by a desire for magnificence. The Renaissance classicism of Antonio Rizzo's east façade (1485), decorated by Pietro, Antonio and Tullio Lombardo, predominates over the Gothic west and south sides. The monumental **Scala dei Giganti**, or 'Staircase of the Giants', leads up to the first floor loggia where doges were crowned and received important visitors, overlooked by Sansovino's colossal statues of *Mars* and *Neptune*.

The Venetian Republic

The Republic of Venice was atypical in a time of feudal monarchies. The first doge, or Duke of Venice, seems to have been appointed in the 7th C under the Byzantine emperor, but by the 8th C Venice was already standing strong as an autonomous power with the doge as head of state. Legislative power was vested in the Maggior Consiglio, whose 500 members each served for a year until 1297, when it was closed and membership restricted to the self-made, hereditary nobility drawn from the city's merchant families.

Elected officials usually held office for no more than a year and a half. The doge himself was intended to be a figurehead, chosen by an extremely complicated procedure that involved votes and drawing lots. From as early as the 12th C, every doge had to vow that he would obey certain rules that restricted his authority, although that did not halt the ambition of more than one incumbent.

The strong institutions of Venice were also aided by the quality and character of the nobility itself, a disciplined ruling class with a skill for business. The citizen class, with its guilds and *scuole*, also enjoyed a considerable degree of autonomy.

Successful and prosperous for a thousand years, the Republic fell in 1797 after Napoleon's troops crossed into neutral Venetian territory in pursuit of the Austrians. The Maggior Consiglio voted 512 to 20 to surrender the city. The peremptory extinction of one of the Continent's longest-standing republics left Europe's liberal thinkers and sympathisers deeply shaken.

INTERIOR

The fire of 1577 destroyed the palace's remarkable collection of Renaissance paintings, but the building still offers a fascinating glimpse of Venice's history. As you enter, take the staircase beneath the southeast side of the portico up to the Gothic loggia. From here the Scala d'Oro ascends to a succession of 16th-C rooms, many of which have carved, gilt ceilings and fine Renaissance chimneypieces. The finest include the **Sala degli Scarlatti**, with its blue and gold ceiling, and the Cappella Privata del Doge, which has a *St Christopher* frescoed on the outside by Titian. The **Sala delle Quattro Porte**, with its monumental doors, has Titian's famous *Doge Antonio Grimani Kneeling Before the Faith*, while the **Sala dell'Anticollegio** contains Tintoretto's voluptuous paintings *Vulcan's Forge*, *Mercury and the Graces*, *Bacchus and Ariadne*, and *Minerva and Mars*, and Veronese's *Rape of Europa*. The **Sala del Collegio**, designed by Andrea Palladio, has canvases on the walls by Tintoretto (each showing a doge among saints) and Veronese. In the **Sala dell'Armamento** you can see what is left of the magnificent fresco of *Paradise* by Guariento (1365–67), partly destroyed in the fire.

The **Sala del Maggior Consiglio**, or Great Council Chamber, is a vast (53 x 24 m) hall, spacious enough to hold 1,700 Venetian patricians, the largest number ever in the council. The room was redecorated, like the adjacent Sala dello Scrutinio, after the fire of 1577. On the walls is the huge *Paradise* (reputedly the largest oil painting in the world) painted by Tintoretto and assistants in place of the original fresco by Guariento. The frieze is decorated with portraits of doges (that of Marin Falier, beheaded in 1355 for treason, has been replaced by a black curtain) and the ceiling holds Veronese's great *Apotheosis of Venice*, surrounded by paintings by Tintoretto and Palma Giovane.

The palace is connected to the adjoining 17th-C prison by the famous **Ponte dei Sospiri**, or 'Bridge of Sighs' (1602), over which the condemned were led. The best exterior view of the bridge is from the beautiful 15th-C Ponte della Paglia, on the quayside, but you can also cross the bridge yourself and tour the now empty cells. The prison was built in the second half of the 16th C to free up space in the palace itself.

Museo Correr

OPEN	The museum is open 9 am–7 pm every day between April and Oct and 9 am–5 pm between Nov and March. Last admission is 1 hour before closing; a single ticket gives admission to the Museo Correr as well as the Biblioteca Nazionale Marciana, Museo Archeologico Nazionale and the Palazzo Ducale.
CLOSED	1/1, 25/12
CHARGES	Regular admission €11.00; children under 15 €3.00; students 15-29 and EU seniors over 65 €5.50. Reduced admission available with Venice Card

GUIDED VISITS	Audio guides available; live guide available on request at 041 520 9038.
DISABLED ACCESS	Yes (ask at Reception)
SERVICES	Bookshop (a small space selling mostly art books), café
TELEPHONE	041 240 5211
WEB	www.museicivicineveneziani.it
MAIN ENTRANCE	Piazza San Marco, Ala Napoleonica
GETTING THERE	Vaporetti 1, 52 or 82 to San Zaccaria stop

HIGHLIGHTS

Antonio Canova, *Daedalus and Icarus*	Room 4
Antonello da Messina, *Pietà*	Room 34
Jacopo Bellini, *Crucifixion* **Gentile Bellini,** *Portrait of Doge Mocenigo* **Giovanni Bellini,** *Crucifixion*, *Transfiguration* **and** *Pietà*	Room 36
Vittore Carpaccio, *Two Venetian Ladies* **Lorenzo Lotto,** *Portrait*	Room 38

At the far end of Piazza San Marco, beneath the arches of the Ala Napoleonica, a marble staircase leads up to the Museo Correr, a beautiful and important museum of Venetian history which also contains a number of incomparable masterpieces of painting. Much of the exhibition space has been designed by Carlo Scarpa, northeastern Italy's most prominent architect of the 20th C. The majority of the collection is housed on the second floor, but those interested in the sculptor Canova and in Renaissance bronzes should stop off at the first floor. **Antonio Canova**'s name is, for many, synonymous with Neoclassical sculpture. His clean, cool and higly polished masterpieces in white, crystalline marble have been widely admired and copied, and by the end of his life he was considered by many to be a sculptor comparable to Michelangelo and Bernini.

In *Room 4* the famous *Daedalus and Icarus* shows Canova's prodigious technical capabilities even at the age of 22. Look also

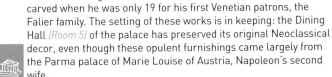

for his charming *Baskets of Fruit*, and for the *Orpheus and Eurydice* carved when he was only 19 for his first Venetian patrons, the Falier family. The setting of these works is in keeping: the Dining Hall *(Room 5)* of the palace has preserved its original Neoclassical decor, even though these opulent furnishings came largely from the Parma palace of Marie Louise of Austria, Napoleon's second wife.

Rooms 19-22 display a collection of the small bronze statuettes which were so popular during the 15th and 16th centuries. In addition to statuary, the bronze collections include many interesting examples of the bronze household utensils that were commonly used from the mid-16th to the mid-17th centuries.

LIFE AND CULTURE
The Venetian life and culture section is the best way to get a sense of the history of Venice and the animating force behind the architecture and art of the city. Individual rooms are dedicated to different themes: the Doge *(Rooms 6-7)* and his hat, and the ceremonies he had to perform (such as the famous annual 'marriage to the sea' ceremony in which the Doge threw a ring into the water, symbolizing Venice's dependence on and sovreignty over the seas); Venetian Coins *(Room 11)*; the Arsenal *(Room 13)*, that powerhouse of the industrial production of ships, upon which Venice's safety and wealth depended; the arms *(Rooms 15-18)* of the Republic and her enemies; and, perhaps finest and most nostalgically, memories of the great Bucintoro *(Room 45)*, the Doge's ornate ceremonial barge.

THE PICTURE COLLECTION
The picture collection is likewise fine; all the works are first-class, but the ones that it would be a mistake to leave Venice without seeing are indicated below. The rooms overall have a roughly chronological order, beginning in the colourful Gothic world of religious certainties with a decidedly Byzantine feel, and leading through to the accomplished perspectives and sensual beauty of Venetian painting in the High Renaissance.

Rooms 25 to *29* show how, in the late 1300s and early 1400s, when there was a ferment of artistic experimentation in Florence, Venetian artists steadfastly remained faithful to the highly decorative but fundamentally old-fashioned icon-like Gothic altarpiece. A very early and beautiful example, now splendidly cleaned, is **Paolo Veneziano**'s panel (once part of a larger polyptych) *Jesus Giving the Keys to St Peter*; its enamel-like colours show Venetian painting's characteristic and unmistakable fondness for rich pigments.

A wholly different artistic language was being used, meanwhile, in the nearby town of Ferrara on the mainland: here, in Rooms 30 and 31, are paintings of a much more modern and sculptural nature. The masterpiece is **Cosmè Tura**'s *Pietà*, which seems to stand outside the world of Venetian painting of the same period. Both in terms of style and of composition it fully exemplifies the painter's penchant for monumentality in spite of the reduced size of the picture (which would suggest it was intended as a private devotional image). The iconography is linked with German *Vesperbilder*, sculptural groups of the dead Christ in the lap of his mother that were associated with the liturgy of the Passion.

Room 32 is the so-called 'Room of Four Doors', which still retains its original 16th- and 17th-C decor. A curiosity here is Jacopo de Barabari's large print of 1500, which shows a view of Venice at the artist's time, as if the whole city were tilted forward in front of the viewer. (You can see the original pearwood blocks used for the print in the case nearby.)

Perhaps the most influential painting of the collection is in *Room 34*: a *Pietà* by **Antonello da Messina**, who had a distinct effect on subsequent Venetian painting. Originally from Sicily, he came to Venice in 1474-75, and left a number of works that changed the course of Venetian painting forever. He taught Bellini and his contemporaries a new technique, which he had probably learned in the Netherlands: to paint in an oil and varnish mixture. This allowed the brilliant white preparation of the panel to backlight the colours, giving an astonishing brilliance to both the strong and delicate tints. Venetian painting was never the same again.

Room 36 is devoted to the Bellini. **Jacopo Bellini**'s *Crucifixion* (c. 1450) is part of a predella from a polyptych, possibly from San

MUSEO CORRER
FIRST FLOOR

ticket office

4

5

45

22

15

21

16

17

20

19

18

MUSEO CORRER
SECOND FLOOR

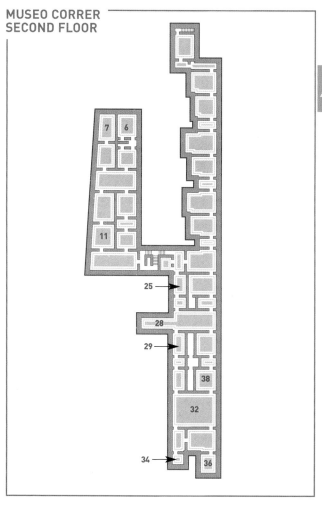

Zaccaria, which also included the *Adoration of the Magi* and *Christ's Descent into Hell* (now in the Pinacoteca Nazionale in Ferrara and the Museo Civico in Padua). The composition is traditional: the central figure of Christ on the Cross is flanked by Mary supported by the holy women (with a group of soldiers in the background) on one side, and a sorrowful St John the Evangelist and the kneeling figure of the Roman soldier Longinus on the other. The low horizon isolates the figure of Christ against the sky, lifting him above the actions and sorrow of those present.

Gentile Bellini's *Portrait of Doge Giovanni Mocenigo*, though unfinished, is one of the more important examples of his skill as a portrait artist. Though an easily recognisable likeness, this profile portrait does not strive to render the individuality of the sitter; it is an image of the Doge, symbol of the Venetian Republic.

Unknown to critics until a few decades ago, **Giovanni Bellini**'s *Pietà* has been dated to the period between 1445 and 1455. The date is important because it places the painting at the beginning of the artist's career, possibly during his sojourn in Padua, where the Florentine sculptor Donatello was working. In fact, whereas the cityscape in the background suggests the archaeological accuracy of Giovanni's brother-in-law, Andrea Mantegna, the angels holding up the dead Christ recall the bronze angels that Donatello made for the altar in Sant'Antonio. In addition to this evidence of early influences you can see traces of that use of colour which was to become the hallmark of Bellini's work—for instance, in the way the artist uses thin layers of paint to create atmospheric effects both in the distant landscape and in the foreground figures of Christ and the angels. This particular characteristic of Bellini's artistic language, indicative of a new interest in naturalism, is one of the first signs of the arrival of the Renaissance in Venetian painting.

Lastly, don't miss what John Ruskin liked contentiously to call 'the best picture in the world...considering ...its perfection of execution': **Vittore Carpaccio**'s *Two Venetian Ladies* (c. 1490) in *Room 38* (see opposite) This is a fragment of a larger painting, of which the *Scene of Hunting in the Lagoon* at the J. Paul Getty Museum in Los Angeles almost certainly forms another part.

Vittore Carpaccio *Two Venetian Ladies* (c. 1490)

The final room contains two early works of a very famous painter. Amongst a collection of Greek painters of Madonnas, from the eastern realms of Venetian influence in the Mediterranean, are two works by the young Domenikos Theotokopoulos, who left his native Crete to study painting in Venice before settling in Spain, where he became justly famous as one of Europe's greatest painters under the simpler name of El Greco.

Museo Archeologico and the Biblioteca Marciana

HIGHLIGHTS

Greek statues of women from the 5th and 4th centuries BC
Hellenistic *Grimani Altar* **and** *Zulian Cammeo*

Museo Archeologico

Architecture and decoration, paintings by Titian, Veronese, Tintoretto and Schiavone

Biblioteca Marciana

MUSEO ARCHEOLOGICO NAZIONALE DI VENEZIA

The adjoining rooms of the Procuratie Nuove house the Museo Archeologico, which has an important collection of Greek and Roman sculpture. Although the holdings of the Museo Archeologico are not the fruit of local excavations but derive mainly from private bequests, they are important because they were the life classes, as it were, of so many of the Venetian Renaissance painters who came here to study, to draw and to admire.

BIBLIOTECA MARCIANA

The building, also known as the Libreria Sansoviana, was designed to be entered by a monumental staircase from the piazzetta that ascends to the vestibule, the ceiling of which is frescoed with an *Allegory of Wisdom* by Titian. The present museum itinerary takes you in a back door to the magnificent main hall, with paintings of philosophers by Veronese, Tintoretto and Andrea Schiavone. The library is used for temporary exhibitions.

The Grand Canal

1

San Carlo
Nova
Salizz. Bean
C. d. Forno
Fond. Giovan
2
C. Larga G. Gallina
3

C. Crisostomo
Salizz. S. Giov.
**San Giovanni
Crisostomo**
**Santa Maria
dei Miracoli**
C. Castelli
Campo
S.S. Giovanni
e Paolo
Santi Giovann

iche
nie
C. Asen
C. Teatro
C. d. Erbe
Salizz. SS. Giov. e

rberia

A

**Fondaco dei
Tedeschi**
Campo
S. Marina
Pindemonte
C. Trevisana
C. M. Formosa
C. Pinelli

**Rialto
Bridge**
Campo
S. Bortolomio
C. Bissa
C. Carminati
C. del Forner
C. d. Dose
C. Lunga S. M. Formosa
C. degli

Sal. Pro
C. d. Zocco
C. Vele
C. del
C. Martinengo
C. d. Dose
Campo
Santa Maria
Formosa

iva d. Ferro
Merceria
Due Aprile
Campo
S. Lio
San Lio
C. d. Naie
Salizz.
C. del Dose
C. degli

larga Mazzini
C. Galeazza
C. Stagneri
C. Fava
C. Volto
S. Lio
C. M. Nuovo
Campo
Santa Maria
Formosa
C. degli

B
Merceria
C.po
Fava
**Santa Maria
della Fava**
C. Paradiso
**Santa Maria
Formosa**
Ruga Giuffa

San Salvador
C. delle
Acque
di Mezzo
Ramo
Malossa
Calle S. Antonio
C. M. Nuovo
C.
d. Bande
**Fondazione Querini
Stampalia**
Corte
Para

C. dell'Ovo
C. Salvador
C. d. Ballote
Pisc.
Zulian
C. Balbi
C. Casettana
Fond. d. Rimedio
Mercanti
Calle
Corona

C. del
Monti
C. del
Gambaro
M.S. Zulian
Campo
di Guerra
C. Rimedio
C. Querini
C. d.
Figher

agazèn
C. dei
Pignoti
San Zulian
C. Angelo
S.S. Filippo
e Giacomo
C. della
Chiesa

C.
Grigolini
Terrà d.
Cotoneе
C. Specchieri
C. Sapadara
S. Marco
Ruga
Giuffa
Salizz.
S. Provolo
Can
S. Pro

heria
C. Goldoni
C. Strazze
Rio
S. Gallo
Calle Fiubera
Merc. d'Orologio
Calle
S. Canonica
Campo
S.S. Filippo
e Giacomo
Fond. d. Vin

C
Fond.
Tron
C. Seòlo
Ramo
S. Gallo
C. Salvadego
B. di Piazza
Frezzeria
Calle d. Ascensione
Basilica
Bridge of Sighs
Calle d. Rasse
C. d. Vi

rezzeria
del Carro
Bognolo
S. Moisè
C. Salvadego
B. di Piazza
Piazza
San Marco
**Museo
Archeologico**
Palazzo Ducale
Riva
d. della
Paglia

C.
Contarina
**Museo
Correr**
**Piazzetta
S. Marco**
P. della
Paglia

S.ta S. Moisè
Calle dell'Ascensione
**Biblioteca
Marciana**

C.po
Moisè
San Moisè
C. Vallaresso
*Giardini
ex Reali*

34
roz
13 Martiri
zi
V
San Marco
arine

in the area

HEADING NORTH, THROUGH THE MERCERIE

San Zulian On the Mercerie dell'Orologio are the campo and church of San Zulian, a very old foundation rebuilt in its present form by Jacopo Sansovino in 1553–55. Some believe Sansovino also made the bronze statue of the patron, the physician Tommaso Rangone, above the doorway. Inside are works by Paolo Veronese (*Pietà*, first south altar) and Palma Giovane (*Glory of St Julian*, on the wooden ceiling; *Assumption*, second south altar; *Resurrection*, in the arch of the chapel north of the sanctuary). **Map p. 34, 2B**

San Salvador The 16th-C church of San Salvador has a white Baroque façade and an interior construction that shows how the problems of light were solved at the height of the Renaissance. It is decorated with sculptures by Sansovino and two late paintings by Titian: the splendid *Annunciation* over an altar in the south aisle and the *Transfiguration* over the high altar. **Map p. 34, 1B**

Fondaco dei Tedeschi Adjoining the northeast corner of the Ponte del Rialto is what was once the most important of the trading centres established by the Venetians for foreign merchants. The Fondaco dei Tedeschi, or 'Germans' Warehouse', was where these Northern European traders were allowed to live and do business. The building was reconstructed after a fire in 1505–08, and the exterior was adorned with famous frescoes by Giorgione and Titian (detached fragments are in the Ca' d'Oro). It now houses the main post office. **Map p. 34, 1A**

HEADING OUT OF PIAZZA SAN MARCO TO THE WEST

Santa Maria del Giglio Also known as Santa Maria Zobenigo, this church of 1683 is a wonderful example of Baroque decorative exuberance. The patron who financed the construction of the church stands above the door (in a position usually reserved for the patron saint) between figures of Honour and Virtue, while four relatives peer down on passers-by. Detailed low reliefs of the fortresses the family commanded appear at the bottom of the façade. The interior has several fine paintings: on the south, in the Cappella Molin, a *Madonna and Child with the Young St John* by Peter Paul Rubens; on the third south altar, a *Visitation* by Palma Giovane; behind the high altar, an *Addolorata* by Sebastiano Ricci and

Evangelists by Jacopo Tintoretto, who also made the painting of *Christ and Saints* over the third north altar. If you continue down the calle (Accademia), there is a very pretty view from the second bridge to the right of the Ponte de la Malvasia Vecchia, with its decorative marine monsters. **Map p. 8, 3C**

La Fenice There is little chance of overestimating the importance of Teatro La Fenice in opera history. The first theatre was inaugurated in 1786 with a production of *I Giuochi d'Agrigento* by Giovanni Paisello and it subsequently saw the premières of many famous works, including Rossini's *Tancredi* and *Semiramide*. Verdi received commissions from the theatre for five operas early in his career and continued to debut works there, getting audience raves for *Rigoletto* but raised eyebrows for *La Traviata*. In its various incarnations the theatre has retained its importance over the centuries, drawing luminaries like Stravinsky, Wagner, Prokoviev and Britten with the prestige of a debut in its gilded hall.

The name means 'The Phoenix' and is unfortunately apt. The great hall was destroyed by fire in 1837 and again in 1996, when it was spectacularly gutted by a conflagration that lit up the night sky all over Venice. Two electricians working on the building subsequently received prison sentences for arson, and it has only recently been reconstructed. Now the lobby has a distinctly modern air, but the theatre itself preserves its antique flavour. **Map p. 8, 3B**

Museo Fortuny Behind the Gothic façade of a 15th-C palace overlooking the little Campo San Beneto is a museum in the house of the Spanish painter and designer Mariano Fortuny y Madrazo (1861–1949), whose fashions and textiles were the rage of fin-de-siècle Europe. Fortuny himself furnished and decorated rooms at the palace with an instinctive affinity with the atmosphere of Venice. They now contain a number of his designs, together with curios and memorabilia. **Map p. 8, 2B**

Santo Stefano Santo Stefano is a church of the 14th and 15th centuries, with a 15th-C façade displaying mullioned windows and a white marble Gothic doorway darkened by soot. The vast interior has a fine ship's-keel roof, but the church's most valuable artworks are in the sacristy: a crucifix by Paolo Veneziano (c. 1348), a polyptych by Bartolomeo Vivarini, a *Holy Family* by Palma Vecchio and three large canvases (*Last Supper*, *Washing of the Feet* and *Agony in the Garden*) by Tintoretto. **Map p. 8, 2B**

The stage at La Fenice

eat

RESTAURANTS

€€ Al Bacareto San Marco 3447, San Samuele. 041 528 9336. This osteria is more than a hundred years old but keeps drawing customers. It's especially convenient if you're around campo Santo Stefano or the Palazzo Grassi. Classic cichetti and the best grilled sardines in Venice. Closed Sat evening, all Sun and during Aug. **Map p. 8, 1B**

Taverna la Fenice San Marco 1939, Campiello de la Fenice. 041 522 3856. This elegant restaurant just next to the famous opera house serves skillfully prepared regional specialties and great wines, and has tables in the campiello in fair weather. Like many restaurants in this fair city, the taverna specialises in fish, gilthead particularly. Closed all Sun, Mon morning and a few days in Jan. **Map p. 8, 3B**

€€€Harry's Bar San Marco 1323, Calle Vallaresso. 041 528 5777. Harry's Bar draws three kinds of clientele: the people-watchers, who like to sit downstairs and watch the artists, musicians and movie stars walk in; the romantics, who prefer a table upstairs by the window, where they can gaze out over the water; and, of course, the diva type, particularly abundant during the Biennali. Founded many years ago by legendary hotelier Harry Cipriani, this is still one of Venice's finest restaurants—and one of its most expensive. It specializes in *risotto alle seppioline* (cuttlefish), *scampi alla Thermidor con riso pilaf* and a remarkable selection of desserts. There's a strict dress code and men in shorts will be asked to leave. Closed Mon. **Map p. 9, 1C**

La Caravella San Marco 2397, Calle Larga 22 Marzo. 041 520 8901. The maritime décor is distinctive and the list of regional, Italian and imported wines is long. The specialties include *antipasto Tiziano con granseola* (a Mediterranean crab), the thick Venetian pasta called *bigoli*, and *filetto di branzino alle erbe*. Closed Wed from Oct to May. **Map p. 8, 3C**

WINE BARS

A wine bar ('*enoteca*') is more than a place to have a drink, although the red and white Veneto wines are certainly worth trying (see p. 187). It's a place to sit and relax after a long day of walking through the city. There's always food available, either a full menu or snacks, and the ambiance is always comfortable and informal.

Vino Vino San Marco 2007A, Calle del Caffettièr. This trendy little place on a snug corner was the city's first real wine bar, and has a well-stocked cellar with over 350 wines from Europe, California and Australia. It's a perfect place for a quick snack, although you're likely to get too comfortable and spend the rest of the evening with a glass in your hand. Closed Tue. **Map p. 8, 3B**

€€ **Vini da Arturo** San Marco 3656, Calle dei Assassini. 041 528 6974. A tiny place near La Fenice and classically popular with the Venetian art crowd. If you need a break from fish, try Vini da Arturo, which has great steaks and creative salads. If you're up for it, go for the *braciola venexiana*, made with lots of vinegar. Closed Sun, after Carnevale and in Aug. No credit cards accepted. **Map p. 8, 3B**

CAFÉS

€ **Marchini** San Marco 676, Calle del Spezier. Fame brings success, and Marchini is both Venice's most famous pasticciere and its most expensive. The sweets and chocolates are exquisite, there's no avoiding that fact. The shop is a new location for Marchini, and you can watch the master pastry-makers at work as they create Venetian wonders such as the plain and crunchy *baicoli* and the cornmeal shortbread biscuits called *zaletti*. You'll have to go elsewhere for your coffee, however—Marchini has no machine. **Map p. 8, 2B**

€€ Caffè Florian San Marco 56, Piazza San Marco. This historic Venetian bar, situated under the porticos of Piazza San Marco across from Quadri (see below), first opened in 1720. It offers everything from breakfast to dinner, afternoon tea to cocktails. In spite of Florian's Viennese coffee house look, was the haunt of Italian patriots when Venice was ruled by the Austrians; Byron, Goethe and Rousseau were also regulars. **Map p. 9, 2B**

Caffè Lavena San Marco 133, Piazza San Marco. There's more than Quadri and Florian in Piazza San Marco: Venetians say Lavena has the best coffee in the city. Founded in 1750 as the Ungheria, during Hapsburg rule it had a guest list second only to Florian's. **Map p. 9, 2B**

€€€Gran Caffè Ristorante Quadri San Marco 120, Piazza San Marco. 041 528 9299. It's hard to live up to a reputation, but Quadri does. You pay for the sumptuous period interiors and the stunning views of Piazza San Marco, but the cuisine is excellent and the service impeccable. You can have breakfast here or a full dinner, and one of their most famous dishes is the baked ice cream, with meringue and amaretto. But many just come for coffee and stylish nostalgia. It was a favourite watering hole of Austrian officers as well as Balzac, Proust and Stendhal, and the orchestra battles between Quadri and Florian were famous in their time. Closed Mon from Nov to March. **Map p. 9, 2B**

BARS

€ Vitae San Marco 4118, Calle Sant'Antonio. A favourite haunt of trendy young Venetians, Vitae is tucked away in a little calle between Campo Manin and Campo San Luca. Stop for cocktails at one of the outside tables. Sleek instead of historic, it's a place to stay up late in a city that turns in early. **Map p. 8, 3B**

shop

Piazza San Marco itself is full of shops, but unless you're buying gorgeous jewelry with deliciously massive gems at **Nardi** (San Marco 69) or **Missaglia** (San Marco 125) then you should avoid this touristy, overpriced area. The Mercerie, **Map p. 9, 2A-B**, just north of the square, is a busy section of town filled with all the best known Italian designers.

Giorgio Armani San Marco 4412, Calle Goldoni; **Armani Jeans** San Marco 4485, Calle Goldoni; and **Emporio Armani** San Marco 989, Calle dei Fabbri

Fendi San Marco 1474, Salizada San Moisè

Mandarina Duck San Marco 193, Mercerie

D&G San Marco 1314, Calle Vallaresso

Gianni Versace San Marco 1462/152, Campo S. Moisè and Versus San Marco 1725, Frezzeria

Gucci San Marco 2101/2102, Calle Larga XXII Marzo; San Marco 258, Merceria de l'Orologio; San Marco 1317, Calle Vallaresso

Laura Biagiotti San Marco 2400A, Calle de le Ostreghe

MaxMara and **Max & Co** San Marco 5028 Merceria San Salvador

Prada San Marco 1469, Campo S. Moisè

Salvatore Ferragamo San Marco 2093, Calle Larga XXII Marzo

As Venice is an international city, there are also outposts of some of the other popular brands of Europe, such as **Bally** (San Marco 4919, Merceria del Capitelo), **Hermès** (San Marco 127, Procuratie Vecchie), **Lacoste** (San Marco 218, Mercerie), **Diesel** (San Marco 5315/16, Salizada Pio X), and others.

ACCESSORIES

Borsalino San Marco 4822, Calle dell'Oro. Borsalino has been a top name among Italian hatters since 1857, when the company was founded by Giuseppe Borsalino. An experimenter and an innovator, Borsalino turned his childhood experience of working in a hat factory into a business that soon became an international success. Check out the classic felt and the famous straw Panama-Montecristi. **Map p. 9, 1A**

Bottega Veneta San Marco 1337, Calle Vallaresso. Coordinate your elegant handbags with your equally elegant shoes at Bottega Veneta, known for its rich colour palette. Bottega Veneta is most famous for its woven leather bags, but the store also carries leather jackets and skirts, trousers and sweaters. Bags will cost you in the hundreds of euros here. **Map p. 9, 1C**

Coccinelle San Marco 4958, Mercerie. Italy's affordable accessories brand offers every kind of tote bag or purse imaginable, plus snazzy leather goods. Their signature bag is slouchy and just the right size to carry everything, and the look is chic, simple and convenient. **Map p. 9, 1A**

Damiani San Marco 1494, Salizada San Moisé. This Milan family of jewelers creates fabulous jewelry for lui and lei, with prices to match. The firm was started by Enrico Grassi Damiani in 1924 and today counts as a premier luxury brand. It's known for its sleek, sophisticated stylings and a fondness for diamonds and pearls. **Map p. 9, 1B**

Furla San Marco 4833, Campo San Salvador, and San Marco 4954, Mercerie. One of the more venerable Italian leather goods and accessories labels, Furla also has branched into women's footwear and is targeting a younger demographic. Bright, seasonal colours and simple linear styles make the typical Furla bag appealing, and they're neither inexpensive nor overpriced. **Map p. 9, 1A**

BOOKS

Bertoni San Marco 3637B, Calle della Mandola. An unusual, out of the way place, Bertoni is tailor-made for bibliophiles. It's a second-hand bookshop, but there's no musty collection of ancient pulp: the selection of antique books is excellent, with many hard-to-find titles and out-of-print editions. There are also deals on remainders. **Map p. 8, 3B**

Goldoni San Marco 4742, Calle dei Fabbri. This is one of Venice's largest booksellers, and the stock list reads like a library catalogue. The fiction department in particular is endless, but there is also a good collection of maps and posters, as well as books about the city. **Map p. 9, 1B**

Sansovino San Marco 84, Piazza San Marco. Just a step away from the swarms of pigeons on the Piazza is one of the best places in Venice for books on art and architecture, travel guides and museum guides. **Map p. 9, 2B**

CLOTHES

Al Duca d'Aosta Donna San Marco 4922, Mercerie. The ladies' version of the celebrated menswear store offers prêt-a-porter clothing and accessories by designers like Alberta Ferretti, Jil Sander, Ralph Lauren and American-born but Milan-based Rebecca Moses, among others. **Map p. 9, 1A**

Anna Molinari Blumarine San Marco 1674, Frezzeria. The Anna Moliari and Blumarine labels hang side by side in this store, offering two slightly different interpretations of the edgy romanticism at the heart of this designer's concept. Blumarine started as a small knitwear company but soon became more ambitious, with the help of designer Franco Moschino and now Rosella Tarabini, who brings a touch of fantasy to the line. **Map p. 9, 1B**

Camiceria San Marco San Marco 1230, Calle Vallaresso. Abandon chicness for tradition in one of Venice's more exclusive streets. The name 'Camiceria San Marco' means what it says: a historic place for made-to-measure men's shirts, where you choose the model and the fabric and they do the rest—and do it fast. If you're thinking of treating yourself, this is a wonderful way to feel part of sartorial history. **Map p. 9, 1C**

Coin San Marco 4540, Calle del Magazen. Italy's high-end department store chain was born in Venice in 1911 and remains a good place to look for glamour, as Italians are definitely some of the world's most fashion obsessed. And unlike some of the smaller boutiques, Coin is likely to have the sort of sales only larger retailers can afford. **Map p. 9, 1A**

Ermenegildo Zegna San Marco 1241, Bocca di Piazza San Marco. Italy's finest made-to-measure and ready-to-wear menswear is tucked away in a quiet corner away from the hustle and bustle. Ermenegildo Zegna is styled but not outré, classic but not staid. A great deal of attention is paid to fine fabrics, and the line has some exclusives, including a staple summer wool that is lush to the touch. **Map p. 9, 1B**

Etro San Marco 1349/51, Salizada San Moisè. Etro brings a whimsical, creative flair and a strong eye for colour to luxury ready-to-wear fashions and accessories for men and women. The company made it big in the 1980s with its characteristic paisley motif. Company president Gimmo Etro is obsessed with travel and history, and the Etro family hasn't run out of ideas yet. The company has also expanded with a home décor line in their signature carefree style. **Map 9, 1B**

Fiorella Mancini San Marco 2806, Campo Santo Stefano 2806. Everybody knows the store of designer Fiorella Mancini—the Doge mannequins outside are hard to miss, as are the colourful and inventive rags adorning them. Mancini is in many ways a performance artist (as those who saw her giant plush rat parade through the streets know) and brings a refreshingly outrageous eye to her designs. **Map p. 8, 2B**

Krizia San Marco 4948/49, Merceria del Capitelo. Minimalist glamour for men and women is articulated in a dozen different collections from the famous Milanese designer Mariuccia Mandelli. She focuses on the adaptable and realistic, while never abandoning the love of design that led her to the business in the first place. **Map p. 9, 1A**

La Perla San Marco 4827/30, Campo San Salvador. La Perla is lingerie so luxurious and decadent it's a shame to cover it up, with delicate fabrics and intricate lace. The company was founded by Ada Masotti in Milan in the 1950s and relies upon attention to detail and love of the female form to carry its reputation. Success has allowed La Perla to expand now into fragrances and prêt-a-porter, as well. **Map 9, 1A**

Loro Piana San Marco 1257A, Calle Larga 22 Marzo. The ultimate in cashmere softness is Loro Piana's signature, with scarves costing in the hundreds of euros. There are also men's divinely soft cashmere sweaters and top-notch made-to-measure suits with prices to match. The brand is so concerned about quality that in summer 2004 it bought the official 'World's Finest Bale of Merino Wool', which will make suits for fifty very privileged customers. **Map p. 8, 3C**

Luisa Spagnoli San Marco 5533, Calle de la Bissa. This line sells fashionable clothing to fit the fuller figure: sizes begin at an Italian 42 (American 8) and go up from there. The brand was at its peak in the 1970s and has since reinvented itself with a younger, more contemporary look. **Map p. 9, 2A**

Missoni San Marco 1312N, Calle Vallaresso. The history of Missoni as a company began in the most romantic fashion, with Rosita Jelmini catching a glimpse of Ottavio Missoni competing in a race in 1948 and deciding she'd marry him. Missoni had opened a company to make tracksuits, but the couple soon moved on. Now Missoni's boldly coloured, zigzag knits take the form of sweaters, skirts, dresses and swimsuits, and the company also makes housewares like platters, blankets and pillows. **Map p. 9, 1C**

Roberto Cavalli San Marco 1316, Calle Vallaresso. To say Roberto Cavalli's snakeskin trousers, white floor-length fur coats and animal-print evening dresses are excessive is an understatement. Cavalli, the son of a painter, extends his reputation for excess to a rich range of accessories, from underwear to shoes to a home collection. His iconic leather patchwork was a symbol of the 1960s, but his extravagance was perfectly suited to the 1970s and since then he has never looked back. A taste for Chinoiserie, operatic costumes and flamboyance mark his most recent collections. **Map p. 9, 1C**

CRAFTS

Consorzio delle Botteghe della Solidarietà San Marco 5164, Ponte di Rialto. An interesting example of fair trade, this consortium, with stores in Rome, Venice, Milan, Florence and elsewhere, sells handicrafts from around the world in order to try and address issues of economic disparity. The group has a view of solidarity as something that doesn't need to carry the baggage of ideology or turn into a charity, but that does have potential as a global force. **Map p. 9, 1A**

Jesurum San Marco 4856, Mercerie del Capitello. Jesurum is the address in Venice for the best new and antique lace, embroidered linens, towels and fabrics. Based in a grand old palace near Rialto, Jesurum boasts an impressive pedigree—Michelangelo Jesurum opened a lace school in Burano in 1860. You usually have to be careful buying lace in order not to end up with something shoddy, but Jesurum is the real thing, and is priced appropriately. The shop carries beautiful work using the traditional Venetian coloured lace as well as delicate whites. **Map p. 9, 1A**

Livio De Marchi San Marco 3157, Salizada San Samuele. Livio De Marchi can make just about anything out of wood: shoes, hats, shirts, crumpled jeans, even a life-sized, floating Volkswagen Beetle. He specializes in the contours of draped and folded objects and a static hyperrealism, as well as 'oversized' art like a whimsical, fairytale house made of wooden books. **Map p. 8, 1B**

Paolo Olbi San Marco 2653, Calle della Mandola. If you'd like to take traditional Venetian handmade paper and leather-bound diaries back home with you, stop by the shop of Paolo Olbi, a master bookbinder considered one of the main revivalists of this ancient craft. The shop also carries notebooks and gift items. **Map p. 8, 3B**

Tessuti del Doge San Marco 1657 (Piscina de Frezzeria). Tessuti del Doge carries beautiful silk velour fabrics hand printed in the style of traditional block-printing techniques. Their mission is to preserve and rediscover techniques that were common in Venice for hundreds of years but are now dying out in the machine age. Their collections, mostly with Veneto-Byzantine patterns, include mostly things for the home, but there is also clothing and accessories. **Map p. 9, 1B**

Venetia Studium San Marco 723, Mercerie S. Zulian. Silk in all its luxurious, sensual beauty can be found at one of the stores run by Venetia Studium, with fabrics and yarns in warm and entrancing colors. Venetia Studium also carries the gorgeous and famous Fortuny lamps of pleated silk, created by Venice-based Mariano Fortuny, fantasist designer and the inventor of the dimmer switch. (For more on the Museo Fortuny, see p. 36.) **Map p. 9, 2A**

GLASS

Murano is where the glass workshops are, along with the Museo dell'Arte Vetraria (see p. 129) and charming streets and canals. But if you are in the city and still want glass, you can find as fine examples of the craft here as anywhere else.

Rossella Junck San Marco 2360, Calle delle Ostreghe, and San Marco 1997, Campo San Fantin. The shop in Calle delle Ostreghe is one of the only places you can find glass from the 16th–19th centuries side by side with 20th-C pieces. Contemporary art glass can be found at Junck's gallery in Campo San Fantin, where the material is wedded to modern flights of fancy. **Map p. 8, 3B, and P. 8, 3C**

L'Isola San Marco 1468, Campo San Moisè. Carlo Moretti brings the island to Venice at his store L'Isola. This designer, one of the 'big' designers of Venice, is known for original, playful glass, with bright and cheerful wriggles of colour. There is also classically elegant stemware. **Map p. 9, 1B**

Perle e Dintorni San Marco 3740, Calle della Mandola. Perle e Dintorni has a temptingly enormous selection of beautiful, candy-like glass beads. They are of contemporary make, but many are based on traditional or antique designs. From tiny specks of colour to huge and luscious bubbles, clear, opaque or gilded, beads are a great way to bring home a piece of Venice small enough to be packed in any bag. They'll also string them for you if you want to design on the spot. **Map p. 8, 3B**

Berengo San Marco 412/413, Calle Larga San Marco, and San Marco 3337, Salizada San Samuele. Forget wineglasses: glass at Berengo is not about function, it's about form. Founded in 1990, the gallery's artisans work from sketches by artists who specialise in other media to create a collaborative final project. Each work is a limited edition and is signed off by the artist. **Map p. 9, 2B**

Venini San Marco 314, Piazza San Marco. Traditionally the top place to shop for hand-blown contemporary glass, the factory was founded by Milanese lawyer Paolo Venini in 1921. Consistently on the cutting edge in terms of both design and technique, Venini has been a name well known in the glass world for a long time and looks set to be so in the future: the factory and store are now run by the second and third generations of this glass-loving family. **Map p. 9, 2B**

THE HOME

Frette San Marco 2070/A, Calle Larga 22 Marzo. Frette has made a name for itself with those who take as much time in choosing their sheets as they do in choosing a suit. (If you need to ask what 'torsion per inch' is, you're still an amateur). If you want the same sheets that they use at the Ritz in Paris, the Savoy in London, Cipriani in Venice or Plaza Athenée in New York, stop by Frette. They also have lovely soft robes and pajamas for men and women. **Map p. 8, 3C**

JEWELLERY

Bulgari San Marco 2282, Calle Larga 22 Marzo. Clean lines, only the finest gems and a continuous quest for the new marks Bulgari, one of Italy's biggest exporters (to the United States, Japan and the

Middle East). Begun in 1884 by Greek immigrants to Italy, Bulgari really took off in the 1970s and has since seen massive expansion.The shop has a glittering and fabulous assortment of jewels as well as accessories for those who don't want jewelry but do want the Bulgari name. **Map p. 8, 3C**

Gianmaria Buccellati San Marco 214, Mercerie d'Orologio. Goldsmith Buccellati, also part of a family of artisans, is known for his maniacal precision and attention to detail. The look of Buccellati is less focused on the gems than on intricate settings of pierced gold with an old-fashioned elegance. **Map p. 9, 2B**

KIDS

Chicco San Marco 217, Merceria de l'Orologio. Italians are famously baby-mad, and Chicco is ready to cater for them. The Italian company is an institution among new (and expecting) parents, with everything for babies and kids up to age 8. Their slogan is 'whererever there's a baby' and in Italy that seems tobe true. **Map p. 9, 2B**

Prénatal San Marco 5783, Salizada de San Giovanni Crisostomo. The rival to Chicco is Prénatal, which bills itself as the world's largest baby chain. It carries just about everything for young children, babies and mums-to-be, with a philosophy that involves thinking of maternity in a new, modern way that is appropriate for our fast-paced world. **Map 34, 1A**

MUSIC

Nalesso San Marco 2765, Calle Spezier. At this charming little music shop you can sit outside in the courtyard and listen to classical music through the window. Nalesso has an extensive list and browsing here is a pleasant way to spend a half hour. The store also recently started their own music label. **Map p. 8, 2B**

SHOES

Bruno Magli San Marco 2288, Calle Larga 22 Marzo. The Bruno Magli collections are known for classic, restrained elegance. The materials are fine, the shapes restrained and sophisticated. Magli is yet another Italian family company, this time founded in Bologna. The Venice shop carries men's shoes, an extensive women's collection and the Magli Sport line of sneakers and casual suede and leather shoes. **Map p. 8, 3C**

Casella San Marco 5048, Campo San Bartolomeo. Casella is where the Venetians go to buy designer shoes and accessories from elegant to sporty. It's lately discovered by the Japanese and Americans, too, but still makes a break from the glamour chains. **Map p. 9, 1A**

Fratelli Rossetti San Marco 4800, Campo San Salvador, and San Marco 1477, Campo San Moisè. The Rossetti brothers began making men's shoes in the 1950s, bringing a breath of fresh air to a field that had been static for years, yet still paying homage to the great styles of the past. A typical Rossetti look is their long-toed loafer, with a perfect finish on the leather and a chunky tassel. There's also a women's collection, with some fabulous spiky heels. **Map p. 9, 1A and 2B**

Pollini San Marco 186, Sotoportego del Cappello Nero. Quality is the hallmark of this Italian footwear specialist, who also produces ready-to-wear lines for major European designers. Their women's collections are brightly coloured and festive, seemingly a nod back to the holidaymaking spirit of the place where the company was founded, the resort town of Rimini. **Map p. 9, 1B**

Sergio Rossi San Marco 705, Merceria San Zulian. This is the place to find seriously sexy shoes (for men and women) from one of Italy's leading designers. High heels, tantalizingly placed straps and the less-is-more aesthetic are what characterize Rossi's design. They're not for the faint at heart! **Map p. 9, 2A**

Tod's San Marco 2251, Calle Larga 22 Marzo. Handstitched leather is the stylish staple of designer Diego Della Valle's high-quality line of footwear and accessories for men, women and children, although in recent years the beautiful leather bags have become as much of a draw as the shoes. Tod's women's shoes aren't cheap but they have a cult following for their sensible comfort. **Map p. 8, 3C**

DORSODURO

The sound of voices over water and the rumble of the *vaporetti* become noticeably clearer as you make your way from San Marco to the great wooden arch of the Ponte dell'Accademia, first built by the Austrians in order to move troops quickly from one part of the city to another. The view of the Grand Canal from the top of the bridge is inspiring, and the light and colour is never the same twice over the domes of the church of Santa Maria della Salute and the Punta della Dogana on one side, and on the other the wide bend called Volta del Canal.

Gallerie dell'Accademia

OPEN

The galleries are open 8.15 am–7.15 pm, Tue–Sun, and 8.15 am–2 pm on Mon. As the queue at the Accademia can be quite long during high season (only a few visitors are admitted at a time), it's best to arrive at least 20 minutes before the gallery opens. If you are not a morning person, the last hour before closing is also good.

CLOSED

Mon afternoons and 1/1, 1/5, 25/12

CHARGES

Regular admission €6.50; 18-25-year-olds from the EU or accredited teachers €3.10. Ticket sales end 45 minutes before closing. Admission is free for those under 18, school groups (participants must be listed on school letterhead), accredited journalists, those accompanying the disabled, and EU seniors over 65. A single ticket (€11.00/€5.50) gives admission to the Gallerie dell'Accademia, the Galleria Franchetti, Ca d'Oro and the Museo Orientale.

GUIDED VISITS

Audio guides available; guided tours available by calling 041 520 9038 or 041 520 9038

DISABLED ACCESS Yes (ask at Reception)

SERVICES

Bookshop inside, with art books, catalogues and small souvenirs

TELEPHONE	041 522 2247;
	information and reservations (optional) 041 520 0345
WEB	www.galleriedellaccademia.org
MAIN ENTRANCE	Dorsoduro 1050 (at the foot of the Accademia Bridge)
GETTING THERE	Vaporetto 1 or 82 to Accademia stop

HIGHLIGHTS

Paolo Veneziano, *Coronation of the Virgin*	Room 1
Giovanni Bellini, *Camerlenghi Madonna*	Room 4
Giorgione, *The Tempest*	Room 5
Lorenzo Lotto, *Portrait of a Gentleman in his Study*	Room 7
Jacopo Tintoretto, *Miracle of St Mark Freeing the Slave*	Room 10
Paolo Veronese, *Marriage of St Catherine*	
Jacopo Bassano, *St Jerome the Hermit*	Room 13
Bernardo Bellotto, *The Scuola di San Marco at San Giovanni e Paolo*	Room 17
Francesco Guardi, *Fire at San Marcuola*	Room 17
Gentile Bellini, *Procession in Piazza San Marco*	Room 20
Vittore Carpaccio, *Ursula Cycle*	Room 21
Titian, *Presentation of the Virgin*	Room 24

Just beyond the Accademia bridge are the Gallerie dell'Accademia, one of the great museums of Europe. The Accademia contains the very quintessence of Venice in painting and some of the most exciting and famous works of art in Italy.

The collection here ranges over five centuries of Venetian painting; 14th-C works in Byzantine style and the graphic power of Paolo Veneziano; 15th-C painting represented by the Renaissance works of the Bellini family and Carpaccio; from 16th-C works ranging from the intense, emotional paintings of Giorgione and Titian to the late Mannerism of Bassano, Tintoretto

GALLERIE DELL'ACCADEMIA

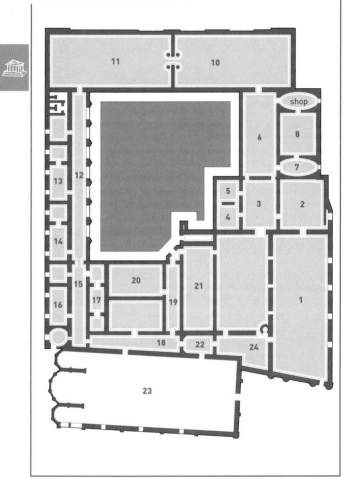

and Veronese. The theatrical 17th C is represented by the works of foreign artists visiting the city and by the Baroque works of Maffei, while the 18th-C collection touches on the great Rococo decorators Ricci, Pellegrini, Tiepolo and Antonio Guardi, to the more naturalistic works of Longhi, Canaletto and Francesco Guardi.

Venetian painting: colour and light

Painting has always been the preferred artistic medium in this city of reflected light. By the mid-15th C, the Bellini family (Jacopo and his sons, Gentile and Giovanni) were capturing the luminescence of the atmosphere of Venice in their beautifully rendered altarpieces. Giovanni's *Madonna and Child with Saints* in the church of San Zaccaria (see p. 162) shows the mastery of the brilliant colouration and subtle light effects that have come to characterise Venetian painting. The Bellini inspired a number of other painters, most notably Giorgione, whose enigmatic *Tempest* (see p. 56) haunts viewers today with its mysterious atmosphere. This love of colour came to fruition with Titian, whose works in the church of the Frari are radiant examples of lustrous Venetian colourism, and Paolo Veronese, who mixed illusionistic perspectives with sacred and profane themes. Tintoretto also left hundreds of paintings in the churches of Venice, working quickly and impressionistically with sharply focused and dramatic light effects. The last great Venetian painters, including Canaletto, worked in the age of the Grand Tour, painting lyrical images of the unique atmosphere of Venice.

PAOLO VENEZIANO'S CORONATION OF THE VIRGIN *Room 1* Paolo Veneziano is the first great master of Venetian painting for whom we have a name, and this polyptych, from the church of Santa Chiara, is his masterpiece. The most striking feature of the work is its complexity, which suggests that it was done towards the end of the artist's career, when he was assisted by his sons Luca and Giovanni (c. 1358). The fascination of this work is partly due to the fact that it so clearly reveals the two formal traditions on which

Paolo drew—Byzantine in the side panels and Gothic in the large central panel. The fine decoration of the flowing robes of Christ and the Virgin recalls the rich gold brocades that adorned Venetian garments in the 14th and 15th centuries, and the delicate tones used in portraying the angel musicians foreshadow that intense interest in colour which was to become the hallmark of Venetian art.

GIOVANNI BELLINI'S CAMERLENGHI MADONNA *Room 4* This painting takes its name from the Rialto palazzo where it originally hung. It reflects the 'primitive' style of the two earlier Madonnas alongside it, which were painted by Giovanni's father, Jacopo, but the incisive line, used to create large fields of colour, recalls the style of the Florentine painter Filippo Lippi. This clear reference to the style of other, more established painters may date the masterpiece to the early part of the artist's career. Nevertheless, in the facial expressions of the Mother and Child one glimpses Giovanni's own very personal, almost dark, painterly expression of humanity—a consequence, perhaps, of the continuing fascination exercised by Byzantine icons.

GIORGIONE'S THE TEMPEST *Room 5* In his short life (he died of plague at the age of 34), Giorgione managed to create a new style, becoming one of the pioneers of Venetian Renaissance painting by putting primary emphasis on colour and paint. This moody and expressive work seems designed to force the curiosity of the observer towards mystery: in spite of the incessant efforts of critics, no one knows exactly what Giorgione was intending to represent with this evocative image of a nursing woman and a storm. Claims that it is a family portrait seem unlikely, and it seems probable that the true meaning of *The Tempest* is an esoteric one.

The key to the work may in fact be Francesco Colonna's poem 'The Dream of Polyphilus', published by the famous Venetian printer Aldus Manutius in 1499, which contains a description of Venus feeding Love while the poet-shepherd Polyphilus looks on under a sky heavy with an impending storm. Yet others argue that this is the simply the first modern landscape painting. The matter is further complicated by the fact that X-ray examination reveals that Giorgione also changed the picture's plan and altered the dramatis personae.

Whatever the correct reading, *The Tempest* remains one of the more forceful images in the history of painting. The air of mystery in the picture is underscored by the colours—the soft greens of the grass, the pale shine of the nude against the white cloak and the silvery light of the towers and city walls, which seem to glow beneath the dark sky.

Not that Gorgione wasn't a brilliant painter of figures; look at the painting just across from the *Tempest* of the old woman. This is a portrait of age, full of pathos. Her scroll reads *Col Tempo*—'with time'—a chilling reminder to all who see this utterly modern and frank piece.

LORENZO LOTTO'S PORTRAIT OF A GENTLEMAN IN HIS STUDY

Room 7 An acute and sensitive psychologist, Lotto has been called the most 'modern' of 16th-C Venetian painters. The *Portrait of a Gentleman in His Study* dates from the late 1520s or early 1530s. Its 'dark' atmosphere is heightened by eloquent details, such as the letter and crumpled petals. Lorenzo Lotto's elegant draughtsmanship and unusual palette never brought him unbridled success—his modesty itself was against him—but he was highly esteemed. As he grew older, he retreated further and further into himself and his work became more and more intensely religious. He died in 1556 or 1557 in the monastery of the Santa Casa di Loreto, where he painted his last tormented pictures.

JACOPO TINTORETTO'S MIRACLE OF ST MARK FREEING THE SLAVE *Room 10* In April 1548, Pietro Aretino, one of the best known—and most feared—writers of his day, wrote a letter to Jacopo Tintoretto that was destined to become famous. It was a time when passionate arguments were made about the merits of

the fine draughtsmanship of Michelangelo and Raphael as opposed to the virtuoso brushwork of Titian and Tintoretto. After extensive praise, the critic concluded with the observation that 'blessed would be your name if you reduced the speed with which you have done in patience in doing'.

In that same year, 1548, Tintoretto completed a painting that would seem to justify Aretino's remarks—the *Miracle of St Mark Freeing the Slave*, which was destined for the large central hall of the Scuola di San Marco. The story concerns the slave of a landowner in Provence who left his owner's estate to journey to Venice to venerate the relics of St Mark. Recaptured, he was condemned to death, but the saint intervened to save him. In Tintoretto's then-scandalous interpretation, the crowd flees in terror, the slave's shackles break open, and the torturers' instruments fall apart in their hands. Giorgio Vasari gives an idea of contemporary public reaction when he describes Tintoretto as 'the most terrible mind that ever dedicated itself to painting'. The work is not as shocking to modern eyes, but this is the real Tintoretto, at the height of his youthful vigour and daring inventiveness. As if to confirm his creative genius, the painter includes a number of portraits in the picture: the bearded gentleman on the left is Marco Episcopi, Grand Guardian of the Scuola and the artist's future father-in-law, and the black-robed figure among the columns of the palace is Tintoretto himself. Completed before he was 30 years old, this work is an open declaration of Tintoretto's strengths: stunning realism, strong religious devotion and intense feeling.

PAOLO VERONESE'S MARRIAGE OF ST CATHERINE The original site of this sumptuous painting was the church of Santa Caterina in Cannaregio, and, as if in deliberate contrast to the humble setting, Veronese used the whole range of his palette to create an unforgettable feast of colour. In the words of the 17th-C poet and essayist Marco Boschini: 'One could say that the Painter / to achieve these effects / Had mixed gold, pearls and rubies / and emeralds and sapphires beyond fineness / and pure and perfect diamonds.' The work draws on the magnificence of aristocratic life in the city and, as always, there is a sort of aristocratic detachment in the way Veronese follows through the ideas inspired by light and colour. 'I paint figures', he was to say to the judges of the Inquisition who, in this same period, called upon him to justify the religious coldness and decorative excess in his sacred works.

JACOPO BASSANO'S ST JEROME THE HERMIT *Room 13* Bassano was one of the glorious triumvirate of Venetian painting in the second half of the 16th C, along with Tintoretto and Veronese, and was the champion of a naturalistic poetics. Bassano had little interest in the pomp of this Golden Age and seems to have chosen his models from among humble farming folk. Painted around 1565, his *St Jerome the Hermit* appears to be a robust woodsman caught resting after a hard day's work. Around him are a few

Jacopo Bassano *St Jerome the Hermit* (c. 1565)

objects—a crucifix, a skull, an hourglass and some books—chosen to indicate his saintly vocation, credible in their very simplicity. Bassano was most at ease when depicting scenes of popular life, which he did with ingenuousness but still with a complex, refined touch.

BERNARDO BELLOTTO'S THE SCUOLA DI SAN MARCO AT SAN GIOVANNI E PAOLO AND FRANCESCO GUARDI'S FIRE AT SAN MARCUOLA *Room 17* No city loved to glorify and to represent itself in painting as much as Venice. The further you go in this collection the more you begin to see great paintings that celebrate the pageantry and beauty and history of the city. The works of the *vedutisti*, or 'view painters', had a special appeal for the throngs of visitors passionately interested in the buildings, squares and canals of Venice. Bernardo Bellotto, like his uncle and teacher, Canaletto, belonged to the realist school of view painting, which sought accuracy in the rendering of places and events. The *Scuola di San Marco at San Giovanni e Paolo* is a sharply painted image in which the reflections of sky and architecture are rendered with meticulous care and enlivened with the merest touch of paint, applied with the very point of the brush to achieve an effect of surprising naturalism.

Other view painters preferred a more impressionistic approach. *Fire at San Marcuola* was inspired by a real event—the fire in Venice's oil warehouses on 28 December 1789—but even here Guardi takes great liberties with his subject, creating a composition that is built around vibrant lines and dramatic atmospheric effects.

GENTILE BELLINI'S PROCESSION IN PIAZZA SAN MARCO *Room 20* This enormous scene is fascinating for the glimpse it gives of the city in 1496, as are the other pictures in the room (there are two others by Gentile Bellini, two by Mansueti, one each by Bastiani and Diana, and one by Carpaccio). The subject is the procession of the reliquary of the True Cross, which was discovered in Palestine by St Helen, according to Jacopo da Voragine's *Golden Legend* in 1475 (this book of saints' lives was possibly the most popular book of the Middle Ages). The painting gave Bellini an ideal opportunity to attempt a narrative work using the theatrical techniques adopted in sacred pageants, and it gives the viewer a picture of the Piazza San Marco as it appeared at that time, with the lost lunette mosaics and, on the balcony, the four famous great horses. Surrounding the action in each picture are tiny, intriguing details of life—laundry flaps on lines, swimmers' bodies are luminous under water, spectators peep with eager eyes from their upper storey windows.

VITTORE CARPACCIO'S URSULA CYCLE *Room 21* **This is** absolutely not to be missed. The story Carpaccio chose for a cycle of paintings commissioned by the Loredan family and painted between 1490 and 1500, was the poetic tale—also in Jacopo da Voragine's *Golden Legend*—of a Catholic princess from Brittany whose hand is asked in marriage by the English prince Etherius, a pagan (first picture).

Ursula tells the prince's ambassadors (second picture) that if he truly wants her he will have to convert to Catholicism and accompany her to Rome to be married by the Pope. The ambassadors return to a rather Italian-looking, but dour, London (third picture); and the prince (fourth picture) sets off to meet with Ursula in order to accompany her to Rome. During the pilgrimage an angel appears to Ursula in a dream and tells her of her imminent martyrdom (fifth picture, in an unforgettable image of the gentle light of daybreak). The couple arrives in Rome (sixth picture) and head back with the pope and a large retinue (seventh picture). The martyrdom occurs during the return journey, at Cologne, under siege by the Huns (eighth picture), who butcher everyone (ninth picture). Ursula and her companions (though apparently not the young prince of England) are then seen arriving in Paradise (tenth and final picture).

In the cycle, Carpaccio allows the narrative to flow within each picture, almost like a comic strip whose frames are divided by the architectural elements of the scene itself—which is why you'll see Ursula herself more than once in many of the canvases.

The stillest and most spiritual element of the cycle, *The Dream of*

Titian *Presentation of the Virgin* (c. 1559)

St Ursula, presents a marvellous medley of deep spirituality and meticulous attention to detail, an atmosphere typical of Carpaccio's style. The scene is set in the serene light of dawn, the luminescent colour veiled by particles of gold that seem to settle calmly on the the bedside table and its prayerbooks, on the soft bed and on the windowsill with its potted myrtle and carnations, symbols of faith and chastity.

TITIAN'S PRESENTATION OF THE VIRGIN *Room 24* This splendid picture was painted around 1559 for the room in which it still hangs—the *albergo* (chapter room) of the former Scuola della Carità. The tender humanity of his shining young Mary and the

theatrical composition is underscored by the stunning richness of colour in the scene. The theme of the Virgin's affirmation of religious faith was a reference to one of the principal functions of the Scuola della Carità, which once a year, in this room, gathered together a number of poor but virtuous girls to secure them a dowry that would enable them to marry. The widowed Titian made the painting as his own daughter Lavinia was reaching womanhood, which may be why there is something particularly intimate and personal in the figure of the fair-haired Mary in her blue gown.

Ca' Rezzonico

OPEN	Ca'Rezzonico is open 10 am–5 pm every day between Nov and March (ticket office open 9 am–4 pm) and 10 am–6 pm between April and Oct (ticket office open 9 am–5 pm).
CLOSED	Tues and 1/1, 1/5, 25/12
CHARGES	Regular admission €6.50; students 15-29, EU citizens over 65 and holders of the Venice Card €4.50; children 6-14 €2.50; admission free for Venetian residents, children under five, the disabled and their escorts and ICOM members. Reduced admission available with Museum Card. A single ticket (€8/€4.50) gives admission to Ca' Rezzonico, Palazzo Mocenigo and the Carlo Goldoni House Museum.
GUIDED VISITS	Audio guides; guided tours available by calling 041 520 9038
DISABLED ACCESS	Yes (ask at Reception)
SERVICES	Café, cloakroom, museum shop; the garden is sometimes used for theatre
TELEPHONE	041 241 0100
WEB	www.museicivicivenezi ani.it
MAIN ENTRANCE	Dorsoduro 3136
GETTING THERE	Vaporetto 1 to Ca' Rezzonico stop

HIGHLIGHTS

Architecture and interior decoration	First and second floors
Paintings by Giambattista Tiepolo and Francesco Guardi	First and second floors
Giandomenico Tiepolo's paintings for his country house	Room 6
Pietro Longhi's 'Conversation piece' paintings	Room 17
The Egidio Martini Collection	Third floor

This powerful Baroque palazzo on the Grand Canal, begun in 1649 and completed after 1750, is a refined example of an 18th-C patrician home. It was also the last home of Robert Browning, who died here in 1889. Today the palace hosts the Museo del Settecento Veneziano, where sumptuous rooms (some with ceilings frescoed by Tiepolo and his pupils) evoke a vivid image of Venetian life and culture in the 18th C.

THE BUILDING

The magnificent palace was designed by Baldassare Longhena for the Bon family. Construction began in 1649, but the death in 1682 of both the architect and his client, together with the financial problems of the Bon family, brought work to a halt. The palace was bought in 1751 by merchant and banker Giambattista Rezzonico, who appointed the eclectic Giorgio Massari to complete it. Work proceeded rapidly and the building was finished in 1756.

The façade on the Grand Canal and much of the interior follow Longhena's original project, but Massari is responsible for the bold inventions at the rear of the palace: the luxurious land entrance, the ceremonial staircase and the unusually grand two-storey ballroom, remarkable both for its real and imaginary breadth: part of the floor above was taken away to give height to the room, while trompe l'oeil on the walls deceives the eye into seeing even greater space. The magnificent chandeliers you can still see were an original part of the palace.

As soon as the building was completed, the most important painters in Venice were hired to decorate it. Giambattista Crosato and Pietro Visconti painted the frescoes in the ballroom, and what is now the *Sala dell'Allegoria Nuziale (Room 2)* was painted by Giambattista Tiepolo, his son Giandomenico and the trompe l'oeil painter Gerolamo Mengozzi Colonna to celebrate the wedding of Ludovico Rezzonico and Faustina Savorgnan.

The building was fully complete by 1758, the year in which Giambattista Rezzonico's younger brother, Carlo, Bishop of Padua, was elected Pope Clement XIII. This was the peak of the family's fortunes and the palace at San Barnaba celebrated the event in grand style.

By 1810, however, the family line had come to an end. The palace was stripped of its furnishings, which were divided among the heirs and then sold, and the building passed through the hands of various owners in the 19th C. It was for a time in the possesion of the English painter Robert Barrett (Pen) Browning and lived in by his father, the writer Robert Browning. It was sold it to the city in 1935.

Original frescoes and furniture, as well as period pieces added later, evoke the charming atmosphere of Venetian life. The *Sala del Clavicembalo (Room 14)*, or 'spinet room', for example, reproduces the atmosphere of the country houses in which wealthy Venetian families spent their leisure time. It takes its name from the beautifully carved and painted spinet (early 18th C). The *Sala del Brustolon (Room 10)*, with its ebony and boxwood furniture by Andrea Brustolon, has the greatest example of early 18th-C woodcarving in the Veneto. The most famous piece is the console, bearing an Allegory of Strength personified by Hercules. The superb chandelier in coloured Murano glass was produced around 1730 by the workshop of Giuseppe Briati and is considered the most extraordinary example of its kind to survive intact.

The *Farmacia ai do San Marchi (Room 21)* exhibits the shop, the laboratory—alembics in Murano glass—and the back room of a real pharmacy which existed until 1908 at the corner of Calle Donà and Campo San Stin.

THE ART COLLECTION

Art in the collection includes the *Villa Zianigo Cycle (Room 13)*, painted by Giandomenico Tiepolo between 1759 and 1797 for the family villa at Zianigo, a small village in the countryside west of Venice. Giandomenico created the cycle for his own pleasure over almost half a century. Many of them depict scenes from the life of Pulcinella ('Punch' in English), including the most famous painting, the oval *Swing of Pulcinella* (1793), on the ceiling.

The *Sala dei Pastelli* (Room 3) is hung with the pastel portraits of Rosalba Carriera (1675–1752), one of Europe's first internationally acclaimed women artists. In the *Sala Longhi (Room 17)*, the lively, sensuous Rococo aesthetic of Giambattista Tiepolo's *Triumph of Zephyr and Flora* on the ceiling provides a provocative contrast to the keenly ironic and critical spirit of the Venetian Enlightenment expressed in Pietro Longhi's genre pictures on the walls. Tiepolo's ceiling painting, with its brilliant and transparent colours and masterful brushwork, comes from Ca' Pesaro and belongs to an early phase of the artist's career (the 1730s). In contrast, Pietro Longhi's pointed little brush carefully dissects the empty customs and pompous foibles of his characters and their world in a series of small 'conversation piece' canvases with scenes of family life and rustic idylls.

The *Green Lacquer Room (Room 18)* has a ceiling fresco with the *Triumph of Diana* (after 1750) by Antonio Guardi. Painted for the palace of the Barbarigo family, it is a fine example of the painter's command of the Venetian rocaille style of airy, refined fantasy, and is one of the artist's only known attempts at fresco. The walls are hung with views and landscapes, but the most striking feature in the room is undoubtedly the dark green lacquer furniture with gilt *pastiglia* detailing, from Palazzo Calbo Crotta in Cannaregio. It is a single suite, finely decorated in the taste of the 1750s, when chinoiserie was very fashionable.

The PINACOTECA EGIDIO MARTINI on the top floor hosts a beautiful display of 15th–20th-C Venetian School paintings and other works from the Martini Collection (Boccaccino, Paris Bordon, Guercino, Padovanino, Sebastiano Ricci, Bernardo Strozzi, Tintoretto and others). Some works are by artists who owe their place in the history of Venetian art to the studies of Martini himself, an eclectic scholar who began his activity of restoring paintings in the 1940s.

Peggy Guggenheim Collection

OPEN	The collection is open 10 am–6 pm, Wed–Mon, and 10 am–10 pm on Sat. Last admission is 15 min before closing.
CLOSED	Tues, 25/12
CHARGES	Regular admission €10.00; seniors over 65 €8.00; students under 18 or holders of valid student card €5.00. Admission is free or discounted for a variety of special categories, including children under 12.
GUIDED VISITS	Docent tours available on request
DISABLED ACCESS	Yes (ask at Reception)
SERVICES	Café with table service, lockers for bags, excellent museum shops both inside and on the street
TELEPHONE	041 240 5411
WEB	www.guggenheim-venice.it
MAIN ENTRANCE	Palazzo Venier dei Leoni, Dorsoduro 701
GETTING THERE	Vaporetto 1 to Salute stop

HIGHLIGHTS

Pablo Picasso, *The Poet and On the Beach*	Dining Room
Marcel Duchamp, *Sad Young Man on a Train*	
Francis Picabia, *Very Rare Picture on Earth*	
Vasily Kandinsky, *Landscape with Red Spots No.2*	Kitchen
Paul Klee, *Magic Garden*	West Corridor
Constantin Brancusi, *Maiastra* and *Bird in Space*	Library
Joan Miró, *Seated Woman II*	Sitting Room
Alberto Giacometti, *Woman Walking,*	
René Magritte, *Empire of Light*	
Jackson Pollock, *Alchemy* and *The Moon Woman*	Guest Bedroom
Marino Marini, *Angel of the City*	Terrace
Jean Arp, *Amphora-fruit*	Garden

Raymond Duchamp-Villon, *The Horse*,
Max Ernst, *Genius of the Bastille*,
Alberto Giacometti, *Standing Woman ('Leoni')*,
Jenny Holzer, *Garden Bench*,
Mario Merz, *If the Form Vanishes its Root is Eternal*,
Henry Moore, *Three Standing Figures*,
Germaine Richier, *Tauromachy*

Garden

This fascinating collection of the European and American avant-gardes is in the 18th-C Palazzo Venier dei Leoni, on the Grand Canal, where the spirited American heiress and patron of the arts Peggy Guggenheim lived from 1949 until her death in 1979. Peggy Guggenheim was the niece of Solomon R. Guggenheim, who established the famous New York museum, and she was a major patron of the arts in her own right. Her gallery, Art of This Century, was responsible for launching many of the great names of Modernism.

Opened in 1951, the Venice museum presents Peggy Guggenheim's personal collection of 20th-C art as well as masterpieces from the Gianni Mattioli collection, the Nasher Sculpture Garden, and temporary exhibitions. The Guggenheim Collection is the second most visited museum in Venice, after the Accademia, so in high season come early or late for quieter viewing of some of the greatest works of Cubism, Futurism, Metaphysical painting, European Abstraction, Surrealism and American Abstract Expressionism.

THE BUILDING

Walk into the shady courtyard through one of the two doors (the one that opens from Calle San Cristoforo is a beautiful wrought-iron gate with large chunks of rough, coloured glass embedded in it to catch the light). Inside, by guava-coloured walls, is the video waterfall created for the site by Fabrizio Plessi, with its soothing synthetic sound. Enter the collection up the steps from the garden and step across the hall and out the front door, going past the gorgeously leering horse and wild rider (*The Angel of the City* by

PEGGY GUGGENHEIM COLLECTION

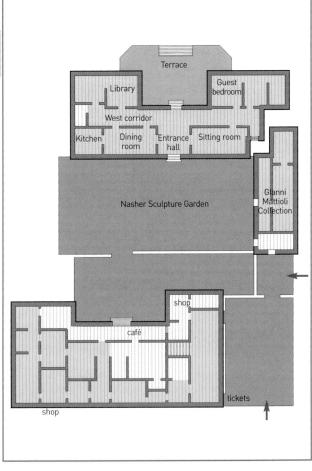

Terrace

Library

Guest bedroom

West corridor

Kitchen

Dining room

Entrance hall

Sitting room

Gianni Mattioli Collection

Nasher Sculpture Garden

shop

café

shop

tickets

Marino Marini), to get a glimpse of the end of the Grand Canal from the terrace of this strangely truncated palazzo with its famous ivy-covered pillars. The look of Palazzo Venier del Leoni is the result of fate, as the palazzo was begun in the 1750s but never finished. 'Il palazzo non finito' was designed by Lorenzo Boschetti with classical lines similar to the Palazzo Corner, opposite, which explains the pillars (there is a model of how the completed building would have looked in the Museo Correr). No one knows exactly why construction was halted.

THE COLLECTION
INSIDE THE PALAZZO

Here pictures are displayed in what was Peggy Guggenheim's living space—the furniture is gone now, unfortunately, but there are photographs in a few of the rooms showing how it looked when many of the same masterpieces were mixed in with the odds and ends of everyday life. Space is tight in the palazzo and the crowds can make viewing uncomfortable, especially in the hallways, so come early. If you can't come early, try to come at noon or at 4 pm, when a docent gives a 10-minute presentation on the life of Peggy Guggenheim and the history of the collection, or at 11 am and 5 pm, when there is a presentation on the art of the collection.

When you wander in, the first thing you notice is the ENTRANCE HALL, which is still hung as it was in Peggy Guggenheim's time, with two magnificent works by **Pablo Picasso** (*The Studio*, 1928, and *On the Beach*, 1937) on the walls and an **Alexander Calder** *Mobile* (1941) silhouetted against the windows. Turn left to enter the DINING ROOM, which was the only room of the house open to the public when Guggenheim lived there. In it are the early masterpieces of Cubism that were there during her lifetime. This new mode developed by Picasso and **Georges Braque** at the beginning of the 20th C caused scandal by taking the soul of portraiture and depiction outside the limited constrictions of form. The appeal of Cubism rapidly began to spread, and the fragmented surfaces and limited colour palette of Analytical

Cubism, represented by Picasso's *The Poet* (1911) and Braque's *The Clarinet* (1912), soon gave way to the ambiguous compositions of Synthetic Cubism in Picasso's *The Studio*.

Peggy Guggenheim's New York gallery was famous, and some of her most famous protégé artists made New York their home. Her collection includes a stunning work by the notorious Dada champion **Marcel Duchamp**, *Sad Young Man on a Train* (1911–12), which in Cubist fashion turns motion over time into a fragmented and compelling image in a similar way to his most famous work, *Nude Descending a Staircase*. Also in the collection is the Dadaist **Francis Pacabia**'s *Very Rare Picture on the Earth* (1915)

In the KITCHEN, which is, unsurprisingly, right next to the Dining Room, Futurism and Abstraction have taken root. Futurism was a truly Italian movement that sparked into life in 1909, the artistic and political brainchild of poet Filippo Tommaso Marinetti. It introduced a dynamic movement, speed and colour (as in Gino Severini's *Sea = Dancer* of 1914) into the fine arts, drawing on Cubism even as it criticized it.

One of the few major masters of the period untouched by the Cubist style was the 'father of abstract art'; **Vasily Kandinsky**, whose *Landscape with Red Spots No. 2* (1913), also hanging in the Kitchen, presages his move towards a pure, harmonious abstraction wherein colours sing like music. Kandinsky's contemporary and friend, **Paul Klee**, creates a gentler but no less compelling and intricate palette in *Magic Garden* (1926), which hangs in the WEST CORRIDOR, just through the door, near collages by Picasso (*Pipe*, *Glass*, *Bottle of Vieux Marc*, 1914) and **Juan Gris** (*Bottle of Rum and Newspaper*, 1914) and a beautiful still life by Braque (*Bowl of Grapes*, 1926). Also in the corridor is an early work by **Marc Chagall** entitled *Rain* (1911), a sophisticated yet ingenuous folk scene. The dreamlike atmosphere of the painting is one of the reasons Chagall is considered to be a precursor of the powerful Surrealist movement.

Across the corridor is the LIBRARY, where Peggy Guggenheim hosted parties for artists and intellectuals and their patrons. Now the empty room is filled with powerful Surrealist works like the

Max Ernst *Attirement of the Bride* (1940)

sumptuous *Maiastra* (1912?) and intense, soaring *Bird in Space* (1932-40) by the Romanian sculptor **Constantin Brancusi**—a pure expression stripped down to the barest essences.

There is more Surrealism in the SITTING ROOM, which contains some of the collection's most famous pictures. The power and enduring appeal of Salvador Dalí's art come from the way his best and most disturbing works combine frightening yet compelling imagery with exquisite lines and masterly draftsmanship, as in the collection's *Birth of Liquid Desires* (1931-32). The other end of the Surrealist spectrum is represented by the clear, limpid and enigmatic style of **René Magritte**. His *The Empire of Light* (1953-54), like all his best works, grips hold of the viewer with its juxtaposition of the convincing and the impossible—here day and night—and the combination of Surreal elements with the cool precision of his photo-realistic drawing style. Holding an uneasy truce with realism are the compelling shapes and colours of **Max Ernst**'s *Attirement of the Bride* (see picture). The viewer's attention is instantly attracted by the deliberately twisted perspectives and the perfect delineation of the half-human forms.

Joan Miró was probably deeply influenced by the horrors of the civil war in his native Spain when he painted his *Seated Woman II* (1939), with its twisted and voracious figure. Equally disturbing yet compelling in form is the sculpture by **Alberto Giacometti** entitled *Woman with Her Throat Cut* (1932)—look for the ugly, gaping notch in the 'neck'. This work is a contrast to the serene, mysterious *Woman Walking* (1932), a forerunner to Giacometti's famous elongated forms.

The relationship of Peggy Guggenheim the collector to the success of **Jackson Pollock** is legendary. Her decision to support him, both by pushing his paintings towards prominence and by giving him an allowance, was in many ways what put him in the forefront as a pioneer of Abstract Expressionism. Guggenheim gave Pollock his first show in 1943, and the eleven works in the collection, hanging in the GUEST BEDROOM, are dated 1942-47. The *Moon Woman* (1942) is an example of a lesser known, but vivid work of his early figurative years, before the notorious 'drip phase', here represented by *Alchemy* (1947).

THE GARDEN AND THE TERRACE

The shady GARDEN and the sunny TERRACE overlooking the Grand Canal are also full of exciting works of art. Most prominent on the terrace is the work of **Marino Marini**, whose joyous sculpture *Angel of the City* (1948, cast c. 1950) is impossible to miss. Here it is worth sitting a while on the canal, to watch the vaporetti go by, before heading back down into the garden where you'll see, hidden amongst the ivy opposite, the characteristic blue neon of **Mario Merz**'s *If the Form Vanishes its Root is Eternal* (1982-89). Some of the works in the garden are on loan from the Patsy R. and Raymond D. Nasher Collection of Dallas, Texas, like Max Ernst's *Genius of the Bastille* (1960) and **Henry Moore**'s *Three Standing Figures* (1953); others, like Alberto Giacometti, *Standing Woman ('Leoni'*, 1947 (cast 1957), and **Jenny Holzer**, *Garden Bench*, 2001, belong to the Peggy Guggenheim Collection.

THE GIANNI MATTIOLI COLLECTION

Since September 1997 the museum has exhibited 26 paintings on long-term loan from the renowned Gianni Mattioli Collection. Mattioli, a Milanese collector who lived at roughly the same time as Peggy Guggenheim, became fascinated by Futurist ideas as a very young man after reading Umberto Boccioni's *Pittura Scultura Futurista*. In the early 1920s he was befriended by Fortunato Depero (of whom he was later to be an important patron) and through him joined the circle of artists and writers that revolved around Filippo Tommaso Marinetti. There are intriguing parallels between Mattioli and Guggenheim as collectors. Each flourished in the milieu of intellectuals and artists of the avant-gardes they were to collect, and both conceived of their collections not as objects of private pleasure but explicitly as a way of supporting and spreading the knowledge of contemporary art.

The Mattioli Collection includes legendary images of Italian Futurism by Balla, Boccioni, Carrà, Depero, Russolo and Severini; contemporary works by Sironi, Soffici and Rosai; early paintings by Morandi and a portrait by Modigliani.

The Dogana da Mare, with the domes of Santa Maria della Salute behind

THE GUGGENHEIM MUSEUM SHOP AND CAFÉ The collection has not one but two museum stores, but you don't need to go to both, as the merchandise is the same—one opens off the café and the other off the Fondamenta Venier, to the right of the gate as you come out. The shop, which is run by the museum and considers itself to have an educational goal, includes hyperdesigned things for the home and sleek metal jewellery alongside the more prosaic bags and umbrellas bearing the motto Peggy Guggenheim Collection. There are also inventively designed souvenirs like the vaporetto stop T-shirts (No. 82, for example, or the famous No. 1).

The museum café is run by the popular nearby restaurant Ai Gondolieri (see p. 82). There's a pleasing view from the terrace into the sculpture garden.

in the area

Santa Maria della Salute The unforgettable form of this church has one of the most memorable silhouettes in all of Italian architecture. Dominating the skyline and commanding the entrance to the Grand Canal like some fantastic galleon at anchor, it is at its most theatrical during the Feast of the Salute on 21 November, when a pontoon bridge is built across the Grand Canal, looking as if a scene from Canaletto had come miraculously to life.

A masterpiece of Venetian Baroque architecture, it was built to commemorate the end of a terrible plague that swept the city in 1630 and killed nearly a third of Venice's 150,000 citizens. The church was designed by Baldassare Longhena in the shape of a crown, in reference both to Mary as the Queen of Heaven and to the mention in the *Book of Revelations* of 'a woman clothed in the sun, and the moon under her feet, and upon her head a crown of twelve stars'. A statue of the Virgin with these attributes stands atop the cupola. At a lower level, on huge scrolls, are statues of the Apostles—the twelve stars in Longhena's 'crown'.

The equally theatrical interior of the church is a spacious octagon designed to accommodate the festive crowds. The high altar, designed by Longhena with sculptures by Josse Le Court, holds a venerated Byzantine icon. On the left is the Sagrestia Grande, over the altar of which is *St Mark Enthroned with Saints*, an early work by Titian. Titian also painted the three fine paintings on the ceiling (*Sacrifice of Abraham*, *David and Goliath*, *Cain and Abel*), originally for the church of Santo Spirito. On the wall to the south of the altar is the large *Marriage at Cana* by Tintoretto.

There is a fine view over the basin of San Marco from the steps of the church and the campo in front of it. **Map p. 51, 3C**

Pinacoteca Manfrediniana West of the church, high above the steps, is the Seminario Patriarcale, a severe building by Baldassare Longhena (1671) organized around a cloister and a monumental staircase. The small Manfrediniana Collection has paintings by 15th–18th-C artists—notably Giorgione, Cima da Conegliano, Filippino Lippi and Domenico Beccafumi—and sculpture, including two Renaissance reliefs by Tullio Lombardo and a terracotta bust by Antonio Canova. **Map p. 51, 3C**

Punta della Dogana From the steps of Santa Maria della Salute, look right to see the Punta della Dogana, the promontory separating the Grand Canal from the Canale della Giudecca. It receives its name from the long, low building known as the Dogana da Mare, the Maritime Customs House. The spectacular construction, designed to resemble an arcaded ship's prow, terminates in a triangular piazza offering unforgettable views over the city and the lagoon. From here you can imagine what it must have been like to arrive in Venice by sea, when foreign ships moored at the Molo di San Marco, at the foot of the Palazzo Ducale, in front of the highest symbols of political and religious power. **Map p. 51, 3C**

Zattere Around the protruding Punta della Dogana is Zattere, the pleasant quay along the wide Canale della Giudecca, which separates the city from the long Isle of the Giudecca. Zattere in Italian means the kind of barges known as 'lighters', and the fondamenta is named after the large, flat-bottomed cargo boats that used to unload wood here. Almost 2 km long, it is divided into four parts, which take their name from their most distinctive element: Zattere al Ponte Lungo, ai Gesuati, allo Spirito Santo, and ai Saloni. As you cross the first little canal (Rio de San Trovaso), look in and you'll see one of Venice's last remaining squeri, the boatyards where gondolas are made and repaired. **Map p. 50–51, 1–3C**

The gondola

The remarkable design of the gondola has been perfected over the centuries. Although 11 m long, they can be manoeuvred by a single standing oarsman with just one oar. Their asymmetrical shape compensates for the weight of the oarsman and his one-sided stroke. They are constructed with 280 pieces of seven different types of wood—for example, the peculiarly shaped rowlock known as the forcola is sculpted out of walnut. The remarkable craft is still in use today, as the numerous ferries (called traghetti) across the Grand Canal still demonstrate.

Santa Maria del Rosario (Gesuati) It was built between 1726 and 1735 by the Dominicans, who took the site over from the Jesuits when that order was suppressed (1668). The harmonious interior has a ceiling decorated by Giambattista Tiepolo with three frescoes. Other important artists who worked here are Giovanni Battista Piazzetta (third south altar) and Jacopo Tintoretto (third north altar). **Map p. 50, 3C**

San Sebastiano San Sebastiano, rebuilt in 1504–48 in elegant Renaissance forms, is famous for the impressive decorative scheme, created between 1555 and 1565 by Paolo Veronese, who was buried here

in his parish church in 1588. This splendid array of canvases and frescoes covers the ceiling, the walls of the nave and sanctuary, the sacristy and the nuns' choir. The ceiling compartments of the sacristy (*Coronation of the Virgin*, *Evangelists*) are the artist's first work in Venice. **Map p. 51, 3C**

Scuola Grande dei Carmini The 17th-C Scuola Grande dei Carmini, associated with the church, is built to a design attributed to Baldassare Longhena. The rooms of the interior are decorated with stuccoes, wooden benches and 17th- and 18th-C paintings. In the great upper hall, or Salone, is a fine ceiling with nine paintings by Giovanni Battista Tiepolo (1739–44). **Map p. 50 2B**

Campo San Margherita It's hard to imagine something more charming than Campo San Margherita as the sun sets, when the square comes to life. Parents bring out the toddlers and let them run loose, while the old folks gossip on the benches beneath the trees and children kick footballs off the historic walls of 15th-C buildings. The campo is an asymmetrically stretched rectangle surrounded with humble houses with green shutters, a nice contrast to the ornamentation of the palazzi. Standing alone at one end of the square is the Scuola dei Varotari, the guild house of the tanners, while at the other is a sadly truncated campanile, all that's left of the former church of St Margaret. In the distance, past the guildhouse, you can see the dome of San Pantalon and the square tower of Frari. Stores and cafés line the campo: **Torrefazione India Caffee** at No. 2964 has coffee and tea and all the accessories, as well as local honey, while **Fustat** at No. 2904 has simple thrown pots that combine solidity with earthy, visceral colours. At No. 2978 is **Emporio Pettenello**, a century-old toy store with dolls, marionettes, puppets and wooden toys on the original 19th-C shelves. **Map p. 50, 2A**

commercial galleries

Galleria d'Arte L'Occhio Dorsoduro 181, Calle Bastion. 522 6550. This 'Gallery of the Art of the Eye' presents works by contemporary young artists from Italy and abroad, such as Tobia Ravà, Andrea Zanatta and others. **Map p. 51, 2C**

Imagina Dorsoduro 3126, Rio Terrà. 041 241 0625. The only gallery in Venice dedicated exclusively to photography. **Map p. 51, 2C**

Multigraphic Dorsoduro 728, Calle della Chiesa. 041 528 5159. Prints are made on the premises of fine art, mainly by modern abstract artists. **Map p. 51, 1C**

eat

RESTAURANTS

€ **Bistro ai Do Draghi** Dorsoduro 3665, Campo Santa Margherita. 041 528 9731. Great osteria with summer seating outside in one of Venice's more picturesque squares; closed Thur in winter. Stop here for one of forty wines and a snack like *tramezzino con speck*. Speck is a dense and succulent ham brined in a perfect blend of black pepper, juniper berries and bay leaves—it has a German name because it's traditionally produced in the German-speaking Italian province of Bolzano, in the South Tyrol. **Map p. 50, 2A**

L'Incontro Dorsoduro 3062, Campo Santa Margherita. 041 522 2402. Just down the campo from ai Do Draghi is L'Incontro, a long-standing favourite that serves traditional (and inexpensive) Sardinian cuisine, with especially good meat dishes. Lamb, sheep's milk cheese and fish are the staples of this island region, as are also the thin and crisp breads *pane carasau* and *carta da musica*. Closed Mon and also Tues mornings. **Map p. 50, 2A**

€€ **La Piscina** Dorsoduro 780, Zattere (just down from the Fondamente della Fornace). 041 241 3889. You certainly can't beat the view at La Piscina (unless possibly at Riviera, below). On the Zattere, with a south-facing view of the Guidecca that grows luminous at twilight, the restaurant attached to the Pensione La Calcina has a terrace in the canal and tables along the stone quay. A short menu and large portions are new, but the bohemian traditions of the café and the looming Redentore church across the canal do their part for history. **Map p. 5, 2C**

Riviera Dorsoduro 1473, near the Zattere vaporetto stop. 041 522 7621. Possibly the best fish restaurant in Venice. The outside seating faces the Guidecca canal, with a view of the constantly-being-restored bulk of the Molino Stucky, the famous mill damaged in a fire and destined now to become a massive Hilton hotel. Terrace water seating lifts you above the choppy waters of the lagoon. Closed Mon. **Map p. 50, 3C**

Ai Gondolieri Dorsoduro 366, Fondamenta San Vio. 041 528 6396. Small and refined, this chic restaurant near Peggy Guggenheim's house is popular enough that booking is essential. Help yourself to crudités while you wait for the delicious meat dishes that have given the restaurant its reputation. Closed Tue. (The restaurant also operates the café at the Peggy Guggenheim collection.) **Map p. 51, 1C**

WINE BARS

€ **Ai Vini Padovani** Dorsoduro 1280, Calle dei Cerchieri, 041 523 6370. Both conveniently located and amazingly difficult to find (it's between the Accademia and San Barnaba), Ai Vini Padovani offers a real taste of Venice in a friendly, low-key setting—a small, dark niche of a place, full of regulars. But don't let that intimidate you—

draw up a chair and tuck into some *cicheti*, the Venetian answer to tapas and a great way to get a bite-sized bit of lots of different tastes. Closed Sat-Sun and in Aug. **Map p. 50, 3B**

Cantinone (già Schiavi) Dorsoduro 992, Ponte San Trovaso, 041 523 0034. The bottles that line the walls provide a hint of what you'll get inside at this friendly, old-fashioned osteria and wine bar. A cozy 19th-C atmosphere wraps you in warmth you while you sip prosecco or crunch into crostini. It's right across the canal from the squero di San Trovaso, where gondolas are made and repaired. closed Sun and Aug. **Map p. 50, 3C**

€€ **La Rivista** Dorsoduro 979A, Rio Terà Foscarini. 041 240 1425. This smart new 'wine and cheese' bar belongs to Hotel Ca' Pisani, and is a place to go modern after a day steeped in Venetian history. The menu is small but the salads, light main courses and cheese platters are excellent, and there are fine wines by the bottle or the glass. Afterwards walk across Campo San Agnese towards the Giudecca canal and stroll down the Zattere in the twilight. Closed Mon. **Map 50, 3C**

Quatro Feri Dorsoduro 2754A, Campo San Barnaba. This osteria goes for tradition, with thick wooden tables and paper napkins. The food is traditional as well: seafood, and lots of it, including the house speciality, tuna in *saor*. *Saor* is a traditional marinade of onions, vinegar and spices, sometimes with pine nuts and raisins, and was originally a 'common' sauce, used to disguise cheap fish of dubious quality. Nowadays *saor* is a matter for gourmets as well, with wine used instead of vinegar. Closed Sun, after Carnevale and late June-early July. **Map p. 50, 2B**

shop

ACCESSORIES

Giorgio Nason Dorsoduro 167, Calle San Gregorio. This designer's atelier carries glass jewellery in vibrant candy colours, including thick bracelets with a rich pattern almost like tortoiseshell.

Nason's jewellery, with its flowing forms, is sold around the world, including at Barney's New York. **Map p. 50, 2B**

Gualti Dorsoduro 3111, Rio Terrà Canal. The delicate, flower-inspired accessories of Gualtiero Salbego have delicately arching pistils and scattered petals of beads, and the aesthetic is a delicate extravagance that would put any debutante in raptures. You can also have sexy slingback shoes colour-matched—presumably to the flowers and brightly coloured sprays. **Map p. 50, 2B**

Norelene Dorsoduro, 683 Calle della Chiesa. These bold, draped scarves have strong yet not overpowering hand-painted patterns and geometrical overlapping shapes. Sold in large squares, they'd look good on a wall—there are also velvets, and cushion or sofa covers can be ordered. **Map p. 50, 2A**

Susanna & Marina Sent Dorsoduro 669, Campo San Vio. These sisters are part of the new wave of contemporary glass design, young Venetians marrying the past of Venetian glassmaking to new, modern aesthetics. The Sent family's work is on the cutting edge, which means they are often copied, but, as always, it's worth tracking down the originals: sleek yet sculpted vases and bright, heavy jewellery in vibrant colors. You'll also see their jewellery in many of the museum shops around the city. **Map p. 51, 1C**

BOOKS

Cafoscarina Dorsoduro 3225, Campiello degli Squellini. This is a favourite haunt of Venetian university students, specialising in English, German and Asian literature and history, art and architecture, travel and leisure. **Map p. 50, 2A**

San Pantalon Dorsoduro 3950, Salizzada San Pantalon. The music-lover's bookshop—it has a broad selection of titles on opera as well as art books, children's books, cards and games. **Map p. 50, 2A**

The Toletta Bookstores Dorsoduro 1213–30123, Fondamenta della Toletta. Toletta has a cluster of bookshops along this well-travelled fondamenta, selling a selection of new and used books, from rare editions to the latest bestsellers. Almost all of it is in Italian, but there are English books as well. **Map p. 50, 2B**

CRAFTS

Annelie Dorsoduro 2748, Calle Lunga San Barnaba. It's best to buy lace on Burano, where it's traditionally made, but if you aren't planning to get that far, you could do worse than to go to Annelie. Here you'll find a superb selection of fully embroidered or lace-trimmed household linens. (You can get a 5% discount if you've got a Rolling Venice card, so enquire before you buy.) **Map p. 50, 2B**

Antichità Dorsoduro 1195, Calle Toletta. Do you love the old glass of Venice but would rather create than buy? Antichità is your place, then, selling antique hand-painted glass beads that can be purchased individually or made up on the spot into necklaces or bracelets. **Map p. 50, 3B**

Antiquario Micheluzzi Dorsoduro 1071, Calle della Toletta. Massimo Micheluzzi is a renowned designer whose designs can be found in galleries around the world. He uses classic murrina and battuto techniques for a restrained, impressive contemporary look that contains a sense of motion within material, somewhat like the play of light on moving water that is such a part of the special ambience of Venice. **Map p. 50, 3B**

Genninger Studio Dorsoduro 2793A, Calle del Traghetto. American Leslie Ann Genninger's pieces are Byzantine-inspired and colourful. She works in glass to create goblets, jewellery and lamps that brim with the energy of her popular designs. (She also has a shop at San Marco 1845, Calle dei Barcaroli.) **Map p. 50, 3B**

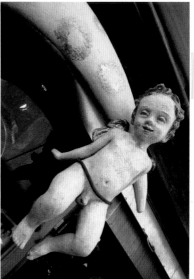

Il Pavone Dorsoduro 721, Fondamenta Venier dei Leoni. Venetian marbled paper has taken off in recent years as one of the city's main showcase items, with designs that range from the traditional to the imaginative. Il Pavone leans more to the latter, with handmade paper in colourful floral designs and non-paper objects printed with the same patterns. It's a good place to pick up small but distinctive gifts for those at home. **Map p. 51, 1C**

MondoNovo Dorsoduro 3063, Rio Terrà Canal. Carnivale as a tourist event was only revived in the 1980s, so most of the masks you'll see around the city are less than inspired. But there's something different at MondoNovo, guaranteed. This shop is the most famous of Venetian mask-makers, known for its imaginative designs and always uncompromising artistry. You pay for what you get here, too, and some of the more elaborate pieces cost thousands of euros. **Map p. 51, 2C**

FOOD

Punto Supermercato Dorsoduro 3017, Campo S. Margherita. Stop by to stock up on bottled water, toothpaste, or anything else you might have run out of. There aren't many supermarkets in Venice—nobody needs them—but sometimes it's a help when you're travelling. **Map p. 50, 2A**

SAN POLO & SANTA CROCE

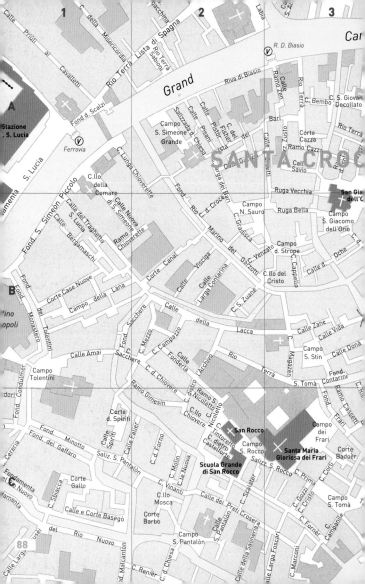

The neighbourhoods of San Polo and Santa Croce occupy the north bank of the Grand Canal, from the busy Rialto markets to the car park at Piazzale Roma. San Polo is home to the most important building complex in the city after San Marco, the great Franciscan church of Santa Maria Gloriosa dei Frari, with its glorious *Assumption*, by Titian—considered by many to be the finest painting of the Venetian Renaissance. Also in this area are the church and Scuola of San Rocco, the latter famously, and magnificently, decorated by Tintoretto. The pleasant back streets of Santa Croce form a residential area that relatively few outsiders visit, but which are the perfect place for an afternoon stroll.

Santa Maria Gloriosa dei Frari

OPEN	The church is open 9 am–6 pm, Mon–Sat, and 1 pm–6 pm on Sun and holidays.
CHARGES	All admission €2.00
GUIDED VISITS	Audio guides; English-language guide available on request at 041 520 9038
DISABLED ACCESS	Partial (there are steps inside the church)
SERVICES	Bookshop
TELEPHONE	041 272 8611
WEB	www.basilicadeifrari.it
MAIN ENTRANCE	San Polo 3072, Campo dei Frari
GETTING THERE	Vaporetto 1 to San Tomà stop

HIGHLIGHTS

Gothic architecture	Exterior and Interior
Giovanni Bellini, *Madonna and Child* **with Saints Nicholas, Peter, Paul and Benedict**	Sacristy
Donatello, *St John the Baptist*	First south chapel
Titian, *Pesaro Altarpiece*	North aisle
Titian, *Assumption of the Virgin* **Antonio Rizzo,** *Tomb of Doge Niccolò Tron*	Sanctuary

Santa Maria Gloriosa dei Frari rivals Santi Giovanni e Paolo as the most important church in Venice after San Marco. Founded by the Franciscans around 1250, but rebuilt between 1340 and 1443, it is

Titian *Assumption* (1518)

a brick edifice with a lively and delicate exterior design, magnificent apses and a slightly leaning campanile of 1361–69 (the tallest campanile in the city after San Marco's). The vast façade, crowned by stone pinnacles, is pierced by a marble doorway bearing sculptures by **Bartolomeo Bon**, **Pietro Lamberti** and **Alessandro Vittoria** (who did the *Risen Christ* at the top).

The church is entered by the main doorway in the west façade, faced in marble. You walk into a

SANTA MARIA GLORIOSA DEI FRARI

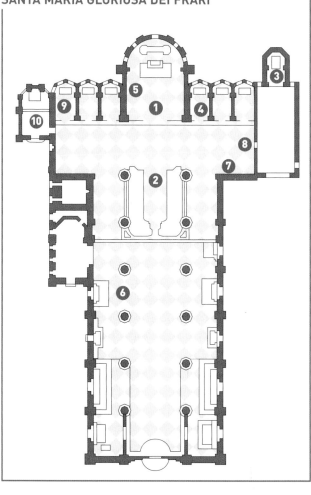

vast, solemn space, with three aisles separated by tall pointed arches. Immediately the vibrant and warm reds of **Titian**'s magnificent *Assumption* [1] are in front of you, hanging like a miraculous and heavenly vision in the spare and monochrome interior of the church. It's rare to see a painting hanging in the exact place for which it was painted, and it's especially meaningful with the *Assumption*, as it's probably the most famous painting of the Venetian Renaissance.

It was precisely the dramatic movement and sensual colouring of the picture that brought Titian acclaim. An inscription in the marble frame records that the work was commissioned in 1516 by Friar Germano, Superior of the Franciscan Monastery; the finished altarpiece was installed on 20 May 1518, in an elaborate public ceremony. At the time it was made, the painter's unorthodox approach to his subject—such a shapely Virgin and excited Apostles had never been seen before—was seen as scandalous; but the stir soon mellowed into praise, and by 1548 critic Paolo Pino could claim, 'If Titian and Michelangelo were one person; that is, if the draughtsmanship of Michelangelo went together with the colour of Titian, one could call that person the god of painting.'

The carved and inlaid **choir stalls [2]** around the centre of the sanctuary are exquisite and the only stalls in Venice to have kept their original position and structure. The Early Renaissance marble enclosure is by **Pietro Lombardo**, and the stalls by a family of woodcarvers from Vicenza, named Cozzi.

On the altar in the sacristy is another of the church's masterpieces, the enchanting **triptych by Giovanni Bellini** showing the *Madonna and Child with Saints Nicholas, Peter, Paul and Benedict*. [3] Signed and dated 1488, it was commissioned for this location and is still in its original gilt and wood frame. The effect of the perspective in the painting is beguiling, and the two angel-musicians at the bottom of the throne seem to initiate a solemn harmony that pervades the whole work.

The south apsidal chapels hold various Gothic tombs of the 14th C, and also, in the first, **Donatello**'s powerful wooden *St John the Baptist* [4], carved around 1438 but repainted in the 19th C. The

93

harrowing statue, showing the saint penitent with a cloak over his shoulders, is the first documented work by Donatello in Venice and also the only work remaining.

On the north wall, the *Tomb of Doge Niccolò Tron* [5], by the Veronese sculptor **Antonio Rizzo** and assistants, is one of the outstanding funerary monuments of the Venetian Renaissance. It is the first monument to portray its subject standing as in life (in the first rank, in the centre, with the exquisite Faith and Charity on either side). In size and splendour—with 22 statues—the monument was grander than anything that had been done by that time and encapsulates the Renaissance ideals of symmetry and naturalism.

Over the second altar of the north aisle is Titian's *Pesaro Altarpiece* [6], commissioned in 1519 by Bishop Jacopo Pesaro, former admiral of the Venetian fleet, who appears at the bottom left with a soldier in armour leading a Turkish prisoner. In the opposite corner of the painting is Senator Francesco Pesaro with two other brothers, Antonio and Giovanni, and Antonio's young sons Leonardo and Niccolò. St Peter and the family patron saints Francis and Anthony stand above, forming the sides of an ideal triangle culminating in the image of the Virgin and Child. The two powerful columns, whose upper ends are lost above the top of the painting, represent the Gates of Heaven. The whole image resonates in our memory because of its magnificent but simple play of richly sensual colours.

The rest of the church is filled with other treasures, such as a fine statue of *St Jerome* by Alessandro Vittoria over the third altar, and, high up in the south transept, **Pietro Lombardo**'s *Tomb of Jacopo Marcello* [7]. Above the door to the sacristy is the *Tomb of Benedetto Pesaro* [8], by **Lorenzo Bregno**, and on the south wall here is the *Tomb of Doge Francesco Foscari*, a late Gothic-early Renaissance monument by Antonio and Paolo Bregno. The first north apsidal chapel contains an altarpiece by Bernardino Licinio, who also did the Franciscan martyrs on the north wall; in the third is the *St Ambrose Altarpiece* [9] by **Alvise Vivarini** and **Marco Basaiti**; the fourth has the brilliantly colourful triptych by

Bartolomeo Vivarini over the altar and a touching statue of *St John* **[10]** by **Jacopo Sansovino** on the baptismal font. A plain slab marks the resting place of composer *Claudio Monteverdi*. The *Monument to Antonio Canova* was executed by his pupils using designs that Canova had prepared for a tomb of Titian.

Scuola Grande di San Rocco

OPEN	The Scuola is open 9 am–5.30 pm every day.
CHARGES	€5.50/€4/€1.50
GUIDED VISITS	English text available
DISABLED ACCESS	None
SERVICES	Bookshop
TELEPHONE	041 523 4864
WEB	www.scuolasanrocco.it
MAIN ENTRANCE	San Rocco, Campo dei Frari
GETTING THERE	Vaporetto 1 to San Tomà stop

HIGHLIGHTS

High Renaissance architecture and decor	Exterior and interior
Tintoretto, *Crucifixion and Triumph of St Roch*	Sala dell'Albergo
Titian, *Ecce Homo, Christ Carrying the Cross,* *Annunciation,* **God and Angels,** **Giovanni Bellini,** *Ecce Homo* **Tintoretto,** *Visitation* and *Self-Portrait* **Giorgione,** *Christ Carrying the Cross* **Giambattista Tiepolo,** *Abraham Visited by the* *Angels* and *Agar Rescued by the Angels*	Sala Maggiore

Just down from the Frari is the Scuola Grande di San Rocco. This was one of Venice's six *scuole grandi*, or philanthropic confraternities, formed by laymen involved in the same trade, who often shared a common national ancestry and were committed to a particular religious cult. These confraternities left a rich artistic heritage, since membership fees were often used to decorate the headquarters with works by prominent Venetian artists of the day.

THE BUILDING

The scuola has a magnificent façade, on which High Renaissance elements (on the ground floor) are tied together with foreshadowings of the Baroque taste (above). Inside, the large halls are decorated with a magnificent cycle of large paintings executed over a period of 23 years (1564–87) by **Jacopo Tintoretto**, whose name, more than any other artist, is inseparably associated with this place.

The Scuola Grande di San Rocco

INTERIOR

The visit begins on the upper floor, which is reached by a grand staircase. In the **Sala dell'Albergo** (where the chapter met) is Tintoretto's vast *Crucifixion* of 1565, considered by many to be his greatest masterpiece. Its power to move left even the eloquent John Ruskin speechless ('I must leave this picture to work its will on the spectator, for it is beyond all analysis and above all praise'). The famous—or infamous—*Triumph of St Roch* (see box) shines down from the great oval in the middle of the ceiling. Set on easels are two small but wonderful paintings brought here from the church of San Rocco for safekeeping: *Ecce Homo*, an early work by **Titian**, and *Christ Carrying the Cross*, which some ascribe to Titian and others to Giorgione.

Tintoretto at San Rocco
The Scuola Grande di San Rocco could be described as a veritable monument to Tintoretto's art, and the reason why is a story that sheds light on the artist's extraordinary character. Soon after the completion of the building, the Confraternity of St Roch (San Rocco) called a competition for the decoration of the interior, inviting four leading Venetian artists of the day to submit proposals. The competition design had to be an oval ceiling painting of *The Triumph of St Roch*. On 31 May 1564, the committee assembled to judge the entries. Zuccari, Salviati and Veronese showed up with drawings and sketches, but Tintoretto—with the help of the custodian of the building—had arranged a surprise. A finished picture, executed with characteristic impetuosity, was already installed in the oval space. Tintoretto offered this work as a gift to the confraternity and promised to paint the rest of the ceiling at no extra cost—provided he was commissioned to do the entire decorative scheme for the scuola. Over the protests of the other artists, he won the commission.

There is more Tintoretto in the large **Sala Maggiore**. The ceiling is occupied by stories drawn from the Old Testament, while on the walls are Saints Roch and Sebastian (by the windows) and New

Tintoretto *St Roch Visited by an Angel in Prison* detail (1567)

Testament stories. The artist executed the cycle in just five years, between 1576 and 1581, adding the altarpiece of the *Vision of St Roch* in 1588. To the left of the altar, on easels, are **Giovanni Bellini**'s *Ecce Homo* and an *Annunciation* by **Titian**, while to the right are a *Visitation* and *Self-Portrait* by Tintoretto and **Giorgione**'s *Christ Carrying the Cross* surmounted by Titian's *God and Angels*. **Giovanni Battista Tiepolo**'s *Abraham Visited by the Angels* and *Agar Rescued by the Angels* stand on easels at the other end of the hall.

Across from the scuola is the **church of San Rocco**, with an elegant 1760 façade. The 18th-C interior has yet more paintings by Tintoretto, two of which are particularly significant. The powerful handling of the nudes in *St Roch Visited by an Angel in Prison*, on the south wall, is a reminder that Tintoretto originally painted his great *Crucifixion* with naked figures, to which he later added draperies. The privileged position of *St Roch Ministering to the Plague-Stricken*—in the sanctuary—recalls that St Roch's miraculous ability to heal those afflicted with plague was intimately tied to the enormous prestige his scuola enjoyed in Venice. It is because of his association with the plague that St Roch is often pictured decorously lifting the skirts of his tunic to reveal a plague-sore on his thigh.

Ca' Pesaro

OPEN
Ca' Pesaro is open 10 am–5pm, Tue–Sun, between April and Oct (ticket office open 10 am–4 pm), and 10 am–4 pm between Nov and March (ticket office open 10 am–3 pm).

CLOSED
Mon, 1/1, 1/5, 25/12

CHARGES
Regular admission to the Galleria d'Arte Moderna and Museo d'Arte Orientale €5.50; children under 15, students 15-29, EU seniors over 65, holders of the Rolling Venice Card €3.00. No charge for Venetian residents, children under 5, the disabled and escorts, or ICOM members. Reduced admission with Museum Card

GUIDED VISITS
Audio guides available

DISABLED ACCESS
Yes (ask at Reception)

SERVICES
Café, cloakroom, museum shop

TELEPHONE
Galleria d'Arte Moderna 041 524 0695;
Museo d'Arte Orientale 041 524 1173.

WEB
Galleria d'Arte Moderna www.museiciviciveneziani.it
Museo d'Arte Orientale www.artive.arti.beniculturali.it

MAIN ENTRANCE
Santa Croce 2070

GETTING THERE
Vaporetto 1 to San Stae stop

HIGHLIGHTS

Architecture and decoration
Exterior and interior

Medardo Rosso, *Madame X, Ecce puer*
Galleria d'Arte

Arturo Martini, *Prostitute, Clown,*
Moderna

Loving Maiden

Felice Casorati, *The Young Maidens*
Japanese armour, garments and
lacquer work
Chinese porcelain
Indonesian shadow puppets

Museo d'Arte
Orientale

Although not a priority, if you have time in your tour of Venice, you might want to stop by Ca' Pesaro, a magnificent Venetian palace on the Grand Canal. Entrance to the palazzo is by a modest door on the garden side, and in the vast courtyard there is a large well attributed to Jacopo Sansovino.

It houses on the first floor the **Galleria d'Arte Moderna**, with a large but not particularly sparkling collection of works by the principal stars in the firmament of Modernism—Alexander Calder, Marc Chagall, Max Ernst, Vasily Kandinsky, Paul Klee, Gustav Klimt, Henri Matisse and Joan Miró. There are also some 19th-C paintings by Pierre Bonnard, Camille Corot, Giuseppe De Nittis, Giovanni Fattori, Francesco Hayez and Giuseppe Pellizza da Volpedo.

On the third floor is the **Museo d'Arte Orientale**, which has a splendid collection of Japanese paintings, sculpture, porcelain, lacquer work, ivories and costumes of the Edo period (1614–1868), in addition to more modest holdings of Chinese porcelain and jades, and Indonesian weapons, fabrics and shadow puppets.

THE BUILDING

The palace was built in the late 17th C for the Pesaro family, based on designs by by Baroque architect **Baldassare Longhena**.

EXTERIOR

The splendid façade on the Grand Canal, visible from Vaporetto 1, is a masterpiece of Venetian domestic architecture of the Baroque era. On the upper floors, a light-and-shadow rhythm is established by deep-set arches and protruding columns enriched by ornamentation. The spacious entrance hall extends the length of the building, its dim half-light contrasting with the luminous clarity of the courtyard, which is gathered around the monumental well-head and enclosed by a terrace and an arcade of Doric pilaster columns.

INTERIOR

Inside, the palace was decorated in a manner consonant with its architecture. It still preserves some of the original fresco and oil paintings on the ceilings, by lesser Venetian artists and decorators. The palazzo was bequeathed it to the city in 1898.

   The city council decided to use it to host the municipal collection of modern art, which had been begun the previous year on the occasion of the second Venice Biennale.

GALLERIA D'ARTE MODERNA

GROUND FLOOR

The ground-floor portego offers a brief overview of **20th-C Italian sculpture** and also hosts temporary exhibitions.

FIRST FLOOR

The first room of paintings represents **19th-C Venetian art** (*Room 1*), while the next room expands into **19th-C Italian art and Medardo Rosso** (*Room 2*). The most striking works are the beautiful sculptures by **Medardo Rosso** (*Madame X*, *Ecce puer*, *Yvette Guilbert*). Rosso, who worked extensively in Paris and deeply influenced Rodin, personally chose Ca' Pesaro as the final destination for his most valuable works.

   Works from the first Biennali (*Central hall*) occupy the grand *portego*. The installation begins with an homage to the founders of the international exhibition—Antonio Fradeletto and Riccardo Selvatico, in portraits by **Alessandro Milesi**—and continues with works by northern European artists. There are modern classics (**Klimt**'s *Judith*; **Kandinsky**'s *White Zig Zags*; **Bonnard**'s *Nude in the Mirror*; Chagall's *The Rabbi of Vitebsk*) and some works from the museum's collection of graphic art.

   A room overlooking the Grand Canal is devoted to the sculpture of **Adolfo Wildt** *(Room 3)*, the Milanese Symbolist artist. The **De Lisi Bequest** *(Room 4)* is a group of modern masters, assembled by an Italian collector during the 1950s. It includes Italian and foreign works by such artists as **Morandi**, **Kandinsky**, **Casorati**, **Miró**, **De Chirico** and **Matta**. The next two rooms are devoted to the Bevilacqua La Masa exhibitions on the **Ca' Pesaro Movement** *(Rooms 5-6)*, which, from 1908 to 1924, brought to public notice some of the more important Italian artists of the day. Especially noteworthy are the early sculptures of **Arturo Martini** (*Prostitute*, *Clown*, *Loving Maiden*), and the Metaphysical paintings of Casorati (*The Young Maidens*).

International art of the 1940s and 1950s *(Room 7)* is represented by a selection of significant works by the European artists **Raoul Dufy**, **Georges Rouault**, **Henry Moore** and **Max Ernst**, and Americans **Mark Tobey** and **Alexander Calder**. The room of **1950s Italian Art** *(Room 8)* includes a large canvas by **Filippo De Pisis**, works by **Cassinari**, **Morlotti** and, at the centre, a large work in coloured majolica by **Leoncillo**. Venetian Abstract Expressionism after World War II is included in the **Fronte Nuovo & Spazialismo** *(Room 9)* collection. All the leading artists are present; the best known internationally are **Santomaso**, **Vedova** and **Tancredi**.

MUSEO D'ARTE ORIENTALE

Rooms 1-3 hold mostly Edo and other arms, including Edo black lacquer sheaths and a quiver with *makie* decorations, and lacquered wood war hats known as *jingas*. The swords on display have both physical and psychological power: more than just a weapon, the sword was a sacred object, the material symbol of the warrior's code of honour, an emblem of imperial power and an object connected with the islands' mythic origin. Highlights include an 18th-C *katana e wakizashi* (daisho), signed Hata Mitsuyo.

Rooms 4-9 are devoted to less warlike items, including a magnificently decorated *norimono*, or lady's sedan chair, of the Edo period. Room 12 holds a magnificent collection of Chinese Ming (1368-1644) and Qing (1644-1912) porcelain and Room 13 hosts displays of Indonesian shadow puppet theatre items.

in the area

Ponte di Rialto Regardless of whether it is seen from the water or from the land, the sudden appearance of the Ponte di Rialto invariably draws an expression of surprise and wonder from first-time visitors to Venice. What is one of the most photographed bridges in the world was built in 1588–92 by Antonio da Ponte, whose design was somewhat surprisingly chosen by the Venetian Senate over those of several more famous architects, including Michelangelo, Palladio and Sansovino. Its single arch, 28 m across and 7.5 m high, carries three parallel walkways divided by two rows of shops. This is where the city's first, and for a long time only, wooden bridge across the Grand Canal was constructed. There are still only three to this day. **Map p. 89, 3B**

Mercati di Rialto The markets around the Rialto have always buzzed with activity. Now tourists mingle with produce-buying Venetians, but the atmosphere remains unchanged (and the quality of food is excellent). The markets have been here since the very beginnng of the 11th C, but the buildings were reconstructed by Scarpagnino in medieval style after a fire in 1514. On a projecting quay by the Rialto Bridge is the Pescheria, a Gothic Revival edifice built in 1907 on the site of the 14th-C fish market, from which there is a splendid view of the Ca' d'Oro (see p. 117), whose shimmering façade is seen like a vision directly across the Grand Canal. The arcaded Fabbriche Nuove was built in 1554–56; the colourful Fabbriche Vecchie in 1522. The Erberia, an open-air fruit and vegetable market, opens to the canal. **Map p. 89, 3B**

San Stae San Stae's splendid late Baroque façade ('Stae' is Venetian for Eustace) overlooks the Grand Canal. Halfway down the church the floor is occupied by a large tombstone that marks the burial place of the Mocenigo family, as the church was financed by Doge Alvise II Mocenigo. The church, now used for concerts, has 18th-C paintings by Giovanni Battista Tiepolo, Sebastiano Ricci and Giovanni Battista Piazzetta—the latter's *Capture of St James* is a masterpiece. **Map p. 89, 1A**

Palazzo Mocenigo at San Stae Costume and Venetian fashion is nowhere seen better than in this patrician residence from the 17th C of the San Stae branch of the Mocenigo family, of which seven members became doge between 1414 and 1778 (and one of whom financed the church of San Stae, described above). The fabulous collection of 18th-C men's and women's fashions is displayed in the rooms of the first piano nobile of the palazzo, which is a Gothic building extensively rebuilt at the beginning of the 17th C. The pieces are arranged in such a way as to

illustrate changing tastes in both fashion and furnishings, underlining analogies in colour, line and decorative motif between these two related areas of design. Mainly of Venetian origin, the garments and accessories are in elaborate fabrics, often embellished with lace and embroidery, and illustrate the skill of the artisans and the refined luxury and elegance for which the Venetians of the day were famous. **Map p. 89, 1A**

San Giacomo dell'Orio This remarkable church stands in one of the few wooded spaces in the heart of the city. Inside are several fine works of art by Paolo Veneziano, Lorenzo Lotto, Paolo Veronese, and in the old sacristy, a cycle of paintings on the mystery of the Eucharist by Palma Giovane. **Map p. 88, 3A-B**

San Polo The old church of San Polo is a Byzantine foundation, and the interior still retains a marked medieval feeling. It has paintings by Tintoretto, Tiepolo, Paolo Veronese and Palma Giovane. **Map p. 89, 1C**

eat

RESTAURANTS

€ **Al Nono Risorto** Santa Croce 2338, Sottoportico di Siora Bettina. 041 524 1169. A lively spot serving pizza as well as traditional Venetian fare in a garden courtyard. The pizza is good, but it's also worth going for *saor* or something particular to the Veneto—check out the prix fixe menu. The owners are young and the clientele is, too. Closed Wed and in Jan. **Map p. 89, 2B**

Al Ponte (Alla Palatina) San Polo 2741, Ponte San Polo. 041 523 7238. Al Ponte is the name of the restaurant, but everyone knows it as Alla Palatina. It's a thoroughly Venetian trattoria, offering good wholesome cooking at down-to-earth prices. It steadfastly maintains an old-fashioned feel and serves big portions of hearty food, which is why its usually packed with students and local workers. The menu includes spaghettis and risottos with seafood, fried vegetables, *saor* (of course) and similarly rough-and-ready wines. Closed Sun and in Aug. **Map p. 89, 1A**

Ribò Santa Croce 158, Fondamenta Minotto. 041 524 2486. This delightful new restaurant has airy modern décor and delicious creative cuisine to match. The garden seating in summer is under a shady tent roof, away from the bustle of the streets. Closed Mon and in Jan, and midday Sun. **Map p. 88, 1C**

€€ **Alla Zucca** Santa Croce 1762, Ponte del Megio. 041 524 1570. The first of Venice's 'alternative' restaurants is still probably the best. Alla Zucca serves vegetarian dishes as well as meat and fish in an Asian-influenced, creative manner. Come for the friendly and relaxed service and the green-painted wooden tables on a quiet canal by a crooked old bridge, in the peaceful neighbourhood of San Giacomo dell'Orio. Closed Sun, Aug and Dec. **Map p. 89, 1A**

Da Ignazio San Polo 2749, Calle dei Saoneri, 041 523 4852. Traditional Venetian fare is served here, and it's good—but the reason to come here is the beautifully shady courtyard, covered by a trellis of vines. The restaurant is difficult to find, stuck in the narrow streets between Campo San Polo and the Frari. Closed Tue, in Dec-Jan and in July-Aug. **Map p. 88, 3C**

Il Refolo Santa Croce 1459, Campiello del Piovan. 041 524 0016. There seems to be a general feeling among travellers that pizza should be cheap, but when you think about it, that's not necessarily a recommendation for quality. Venice's most luxurious pizzeria has tables outside in a pretty little square overlooking the church of San Giacomo dell'Orio. Closed Mon, in Dec and Feb. **Map p. 88, 3A**

Osteria da Fiore San Polo 2202a, Calle dello Scaleter, 041 721308. Chef Mara Martin is a Michelin star winner and her approach to cuisine is based on the internationality of Venetian history and the recipes she learned at her grandmother's knee. Da Fiore is one of the 'big' restaurants of Venice, with a high reputation and prices to match. Freshness and balance are the keywords here, and elegant simplicity. Closed Sun, Mon, a few days around Christmas and in Aug. **Map p. 89, 1B**

WINE BARS

€ **Bancogiro** San Polo 122, Campo San Giacometto. 041 523 2061. One street away from the busy Rialto markets is Bancogiro, a sweet spot of relaxation for a summer afternoon. There's a wonderful view across the Grand Canal of the Fondaco dei Tedeschi (see p. 34).The menu is short, but light and exquisite, and the wine list

is long. It's a perfect place for a slow meal in good company, or with a good book. It's also open late—for Venice, that is—until 1 am. Closed Sun evening and Mon. **Map p. 89, 3B**

CAFÉS

€ **Caffè dei Frari** San Polo 2564, Fondamenta dei Frari. This cosy bar and café has a strong local following (it's also called Caffè Toppo, for those in the know) and takes its coffee very seriously. You can also drink a classic spritz here. (The spritz, Venice's most characteristic aperitif, is white wine, Campari and soda water.) An intimate little place, dei Frari is a pleasant stop, but don't plan to eat more than a sandwich here. Closed Sun. **Map p. 88, 3C**

Do Mori San Polo 429, Calle dei Do Mori. The famous hanging copper pots of Do Mori are described in every travel guide, but it still retains its rough and appealing ambience. The bar offers a feast of *cicheti* and *francobolli* (postage stamp) sandwiches and is always full of an evening. Stop by for an excuse to drink and snack. Closed Sun. **Map p. 89, 2B**

shop

ACCESSORIES

Balocoloc Santa Croce 2134, Calle Longa. Balocoloc is known for its affordable handmade hats, but is also a good place to go for masks and other Carnevale items. They also make a type of heavy cloak known as a *tabarro*, with a full sweep and heavy drape—the close weave of the cloth makes it naturally waterproof. **Map p. 80, 3B**

Hibiscus San Polo 1060, Calle de l'Ogio. Gorgeous colourful handmade bags, ceramics, jewellery and scarves abound at Hibiscus. Pearls and other rough stones make a change from the usual glass and silk, and there's such an abundance of beautiful objects that one can forget about the tourist sites and end up spending the day here! **Map p. 89, 2B**

Il Mercante di Sabbia San Polo 2600, Rio terra' dei Frari. The 'Merchant of the Sands' sells clutch bags covered in square pieces of shell, of inspired and sexy design, and other ethnically postmodern items. The international look is more traditional than you might realize, considering that Venice was the crossroads of world trade for most of its history. **Map p. 88, 3C**

Piaroa San Polo 1247,Campo Sant'Aponal. Almost impossible to find, but worth it when you do, Piaroa carries vintage clothing and current designs by the shop's owner and Carnevale items for hire. In an interesting twist, the Piaroa are an indigenous people of Venezuela—that is, 'Little Venice', named by Columbus on a whim because the houses reminded him of the Venetians'. **Map p. 89, 2B**

Valeria Bellinaso San Polo 1226, Campo Sant'Aponal. The bags and shoes made by former industrial designer Bellinaso are so deliciously luxe that you want to eat them. She uses classic, traditional Venetian materials—soft and heavy velvet, rich and glowing silk—to make chic, inventive and unusual designs, with pleats and tucks in unusual places. Prices are high, but every Bellinaso bag or scarf is sure to attract lots of attention and a multitude of compliments. **Map p. 89, 2B**

BOOKS

Cluva Santa Croce 197, Tolentini. You have to go inside the Faculty of Architecture to find this bookshop, specialising in fine arts, industrial design and, of course, architecture. **Map p. 88, 1B**

CRAFTS

Attombri San Polo 74, Sottoportico dei Orefici. Brothers Sefano and Daniele Attombri craft their high fashion, Byzantine-influenced jewellery using Murano glass. Their work has been used to accessorise Dolce & Gabbana and the fine quality of their materials, including antique glass and silver and gold wire, is reflected in their prices. **Map p. 89, 3B**

Bambolandia San Polo 1462, Calle Madonnetta. Beatrice Perini, a Venice native, makes top-of-the-line porcelain dolls, including of traditional figures like Pinocchio. Perini's dolls have faces that are uncannily realistic and expressive, and her limited editions run from the hundreds of euros to the thousands. **Map p. 89, 1C**

Gilberto Penzo San Polo 2681, Calle 2 dei Saoneri. If you dream of taking a gondola, sandolo, toppo or vaporetto home in your suitcase, this modelmaker has the thing for you. Penzo is from a family of shipbuilders and his passion for gondolas and other Venetian boats has made him spend years researching old plans and listening to the few remaining gondola makers. He also sells inexpensive kits for the do-it-yourself shipbuilder. **Map p. 88, 3C**

Polliero San Polo 2995, Campo dei Frari. This is the place to buy fine, if pricey, leather-bound diaries, frames, notebooks and photo albums. **Map p. 88, 3C**

FOOD & WINE

Aliani San Polo 654/5, Ruga Rialto. If you need a break from restaurants (or your budget is getting a little fatigued), Aliani is good place to go for sandwich stuff. This traditional grocery stocks a wide selection of cold meats and cheeses, plus fun little savouries like tapenades and sun-dried tomatoes. **Map p. 89, 2B**

Mascari San Polo 381, Ruga degli Speziali. The last of the Venetian *speziali* (spice merchants) sells mushrooms, dried fruits and nuts, wine and olive oil from all parts of Italy, in addition to exotic spices. Shops like this were once very common in the city, but wider availability of goods has made them redundant. **Map p. 89, 3B**

Mercati del Rialto San Polo, at the Ponte di Rialto. There is no place like the open markets at the foot of the Rialto bridge for an experience of Venetian life. And, besides, the produce, fish and meat are wonderful. There have been markets here from the medieval times, selling the same sorts of things and providing a sense of continuity in this ancient city. **Map p. 89, 3B**

THE HOME

Dalla Venezia Santa Croce 2074, Calle Pesaro. There's something about Venice that seems to call for gold, and the artisans of Dalla Venezia know that. Here gilt frames are made using the traditional Venetian gold leaf technique. **Map p. 89, 1A**

Luigi Bevilacqua Santa Croce 1320, Calle de la Comare. The silk brocades, damasks and velvets at Bevilaqua, a 200-year-old *tessitura*, or weavers' shop, are astounding. A feast of sensual colour, some are hand woven on 17th-C looms to ensure strict adherence to tradition. The handmade brocades and velvets in particular are gorgeous, and so is the *brocatelle*, or 'little brocade', a silk and linen blend with a pattern in relief. **Map p. 88, 2A**

JEWELLERY

Laberintho San Polo 2236, Calle del Scaleter. A tiny but fascinating shop run by a group of young goldsmiths who create their own designs but will also work to your specifications. Their look is modern and angular, and they favour inlays of precious stones and other materials. **Map p. 89, 1B**

CANNAREGIO & AROUND THE LAGOON

Campo
di S. Alvise
Sant'Alvise

1

C. La

C. d. Capitello

C. d. Muneghe

Sensa

C. Malvasia

C. Cattari

C. Zuddo

Rmesini

Ramo
Corditina

C. d. Forno

Ormesini

Nuove

Omesini

Rio Terra Farsetti

Calle dell'Aseo

R. Terra d. Cristo

C. d. Cristo

Rio Terra
d. la Chiesa

Campo
S. Marcuola

S. Marcuola

urchi

OCE

zier

C. d. Forno

C. d. Tintor

C. Colombo

Caminari

C. Grue

C. d. Tron

C. d. Forno

**Palazzo
Mocenigo**

Salizzada

C. Stae

Pond. Rimpetto Mocenigo

Fond.
Pesaro

C. del Ravano

2

C. Gradisca

Fond. Madonna dell'Orto

C. Loredan

C. Brazzo

Fondamenta

C. Longo

Fondamenta

C.llo
Piave

Piave

C. Larga

dei

della

Orto

Madonna dell'Orto

C. della Madonna
dell'Orto

C. dei Mori

Mori

Fond. Moro

Fond. Canal F. Diego

Rio Terrà d. Maddalena

C. Vendramin

Vendramin

C.
Vendramin

C. d. Cristo

C.
Malvasia

Corte
Erizzo

Via
V.

C. d.
Forno

C. Correr
Emanuele

C. d.
Forno

C.ter d. Olio

C.te
Barbaro

V S. Stae

Campo
S. Stae

San Stae

Ca' Pesaro

C. Pesaro

C. Corner

C. d. Rosa

3

V Orto

A

Fond. Gasparo Contarini

C.te d. Muti

Corte Vecchia

Fond.
dell'Abbazia

C. di Trevisan

Misericordia

C. Larga Lezze

B

Fond. Moro

C. Zancani

Fond.
Vendramin

Fond.
Vendramin

Fond. Trapolin

Fond. della
Misericordia

C. Chiesa

Fond. Former

C. Noal

C.
Salamon

Fond. S. Felice

Campo
S. Felice

C. d. Chiesa

C. d. Stua

C. Larga
Doge Priuli

C. S.
Felice

Strada

Calle

dell'

C. Pistor

C. d. Forno

C. Zotti

C. d. Vele

C

**Ca d'Oro
Galleria
Franchetti**

C. d. Oro

Campo

osca

V Ca d'Oro

Fondame
della Riv

NNAREGIO

Grand

The sestiere of Cannaregio occupies the northwestern part of the city, between the Grand Canal and the Lagoon. From the church of the Scalzi, next to the train station, you can wander amid busy calli and quiet campi to the Ghetto, one of the prettier areas of the city and one with a fascinating and well-documented history. There are also four important churches—the Madonna dell'Orto, the Gesuiti, Santa Maria dei Miracoli, and San Giovanni Crisostomo—and the splendid Ca' d'Oro, a fantastical Gothic mansion now housing a beautiful collection of paintings, sculpture and applied arts. Above all, Cannaregio gives a delightful vision of a true Venetians' Venice, since it is a quiet and residential area largely ignored by tourism.

If time allows, a visit to Murano, Burano and Torcello, the three inhabited islands in the lagoon between Venice and the mainland, should never be missed. Although it may take the most part of day to visit all three islands briefly, it is nonetheless a wonderfully rewarding—and not difficult—excursion. You will come closer to the reality of Venetian life out of the glare of mass tourism, and the journey offers a great variety of views of the lagoon and of different kinds of architecture and atmosphere. Without such a journey across the lagoon it is hard truly to understand the extraordinary setting of this extraordinary city.

Murano and Burano are known for their glass and lace, while Torcello, now a romantic place with a village with fewer than 50 inhabitants, is famous for its great and ancient cathedral, whose sheer splendour might alone justify the journey.

Museo della Comunità Ebraica

OPEN	The museum is open 10 am–6 pm, Sun-Fri.
CLOSED	Sat & Jewish holidays
CHARGES	Regular admission € 8.00, students or holders of the Venice Card €6.50
GUIDED VISITS	Included in the price is a tour of the Ghetto's synagogues, in Italian and English, from 10.30 am–4.30 pm, every hour on the half hour.
DISABLED ACCESS	None
SERVICES	Museum shop, with an extensive multilingual selection of books, and kosher café
TELEPHONE	041 715 359
WEB	www.museoebraico.it
MAIN ENTRANCE	Cannaregio 2902B, Campo del Ghetto Nuovo
GETTING THERE	Vaporetto 1 or 82 to San Marcuola stop

HIGHLIGHTS

Antique silver and texts	Museum
Synagogues	Guided tour

The collections of this small museum of Jewish history and culture include fabrics and silver, an assortment of *Ketubbòt* (marriage contracts), liturgical objects and other interesting examples of Venetian Jewish art of the 17th to the 19th centuries. There is also information on the plight of Venetian Jews during the Holocaust.

The best thing about the museum, however, is that it is not limited to the four walls of the building that contains it. Throughout the day, docents offer guided tours of the ghetto and of three of its synagogues, turning the whole place into a fascinating open-air display.

Jewish settlement on Venetian lands began long ago, with archaeological and documentary evidence attesting to the presence of Jewish merchants at Aquileia, Grado and Concordia as far back as the 4th or 5th centuries. These early Ashkenazi settlers, who came from the Eastern Mediterranean and Central Europe, were joined after 1492 by Sephardim expelled from Spain and Portugal.

Small communities first arose on the Venetian mainland at Padua, Treviso, Bassano and Conegliano. Some of these early colonists came to the capital, where they lived in perennial uncertainty due to the city's habit of granting and withdrawing residence permits.

A decree of 29 March 1516 established that Jews could live and work permanently in Venice only around the Campo del Ghetto Nuovo in the parish of San Girolamo, making this tiny, water-ringed neighbourhood the oldest historically documented ghetto in the world. The site was originally occupied by a foundry—or, in Venetian dialect, a *getto*.

Venice's Jews had a relatively good relationship, for the time, with the Republic. They had religious freedom, but were obliged to follow rules that limited them to the professions of medicine, money-lending and the trading of used clothing. They lived in the ghetto until 1797, when Napoleon demolished the gates (the hinges are still visible), which accounts for the unusual height of the ghetto's buildings—they tower to a teetering height of seven levels, far above any of the surrounding buildings. There were enough residents that the ghetto had to expand in 1541 and again in 1633 to include some of the areas around the tiny campo, the Ghetto Vecchio and the Ghetto Nuovissimo.

Today Venice's small island ghetto is one of the more fascinating neighbourhoods in Europe, with five 16-th and 17th-C synagogues clustered together.

The most sumptuous of the synagogues—each one is built into an existing building—is the **Scuola Levantina**, in the Ghetto Vecchio, established in 1538 and remodelled in the 17th C. It was a Sephardic synagogue for a wealthy community and was decorated, like all the synagogues, in high style by a Gentile—possibly to a design by Baldassarre Longhena—as Jews were barred from craft guilds. The oldest of the synagogues is the **Scuola Grande Tedesco**, established in 1528 by the Ashkenazi community and redecorated in carved gilt wood during the Baroque era.

Even if very few Jews live in Venice today (about 500 according to a recent estimate, with only 30 in the area of the ghetto itself and ten of those 30 in the retirement home on the campo), the community works hard to preserve its traditions and artistic heritage and to make its history and culture known.

Galleria Franchetti/ Ca d'Oro

OPEN	The gallery is open 8.15 am–2 pm, Mon (ticket office 8.15 am–1.30 pm), and Tue-Sun 8.15 am–7.15 pm (ticket office 8.15 am–6.45 pm).
CLOSED	1/1, 1/5, 25/12
CHARGES	Regular admission €5.00; 18-25 year-olds from the European Union and accredited teachers €2.50. No charge for those under 18, school groups (participants must be listed on school letterhead), accredited journalists, disabled and their escorts and EU seniors over 65. Combined ticket allows entry to the Gallerie dell'Accademia and Museo Orientale €11/€5.50.
GUIDED VISITS	Audioguides and English text available; English-language tours available on request at 041 520 0345
DISABLED ACCESS	Yes (ask at Reception)
SERVICES	Cloakroom, museum shop
TELEPHONE	041 522 2249 (for reservations 041 520 0345)
WEB	www.cadoro.org
MAIN ENTRANCE	Cannaregio 3932
GETTING THERE	Vaporetto 1 to Ca' d'Oro stop

GALLERIA FRANCHETTI/CA D'ORO

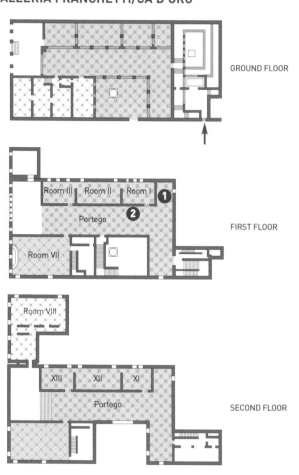

GROUND FLOOR

FIRST FLOOR

SECOND FLOOR

HIGHLIGHTS

Andrea Mantegna, *St Sebastian*	First-floor portego
Tullio Lombardo, *Double Portrait*	
Giorgione and Titian's Fresco fragments from the Fondaco dei Tedeschi	Second-floor portego

The Ca' d'Oro (or 'Golden House') is, on the outside, the most striking and sumptuous late Gothic private mansion in the city. It takes its name from the splendid gilt decorations that once adorned its still magnificent façade, facing the Grand Canal. The palace is now an interesting museum displaying former owner Baron Giorgio Franchetti's outstanding art collection, which covers the 15th to the 18th C and includes not only paintings but Venetian marbles, bronzes and ceramics. Don't omit, before leaving, to take a stroll outside in the small secret garden and along the stunning canal-front portico.

THE BUILDING

The palace was built between 1421 and 1440 for Marino Contarini, a rich Venetian merchant, over the foundations of an older palace.

The plan follows that of the earlier building, with rooms arranged around a central *portego*, or gallery, but an innovative twist is represented by the three stacked *loggias*—the simplest is at the water level, and the decoration becomes more elaborate on subsequent levels. The roofline, with its alternating large and small pinnacles on the cornice, makes up a last, aerial screen, and the entire façade is faced with lightly veined marbles in subtle pastel tones punctuated by red Verona marble. On the land side a high battlemented wall separates the courtyard from the calle, which is reached through an imposing doorway under an angel bearing the Contarini emblem.

Purchased in 1894 by Baron Giorgio Franchetti, the Ca' d'Oro was renovated (the ground-floor mosaic, based on the mosaics of St Mark's, dates from this period) and then donated to the state, which has expanded the gallery's collection.

Andrea Mantegna *St Sebastian*

FIRST FLOOR
Portego

Franchetti had a faux chapel built to accommodate what he rightly considered the most important work in his collection, **Andrea Mantegna**'s *St Sebastian* [1]. The subject of St Sebastian seems to have held some mysterious fascination for Mantegna, who painted at least three other versions (one is at the Accademia, one in Paris and one in Vienna), but his most powerful treatment is this Ca' d'Oro painting.

The style is certainly that of the his later years (1490–1500), filled with symbolic nuance: the tortured line of the drapery accentuates the idea of Christian suffering in the name of faith, and the ample use of purple-grey 'bruise' tones emphasizes the saint's human agony. The perspective rendering of anatomy (notice the foot that steps out of the frame at the bottom of the painting) is as sophisticated as that of the artist's most famous painting, the *Dead Christ*, now in Milan's Pinacoteca di Brera.

Other outstanding works in this room are **Tullio Lombardo**'s *Double Portrait* [2], with its luxuriant heads of curly hair. The bronze relief *Stories of the Cross* by Andrea Briosco ('Il Riccio') were saved from the destroyed church of Santa Maria dei Servi.

Jacopo Sansovino's *Madonna col Bambino* is a relief in white Carrara marble from the high altar of Palladio's church of the Zitelle on the Giudecca (where it has been replaced by a plaster cast), while Tullio Lombardo's *Last Supper* is a marble relief made for an altar of Santa Maria dei Miracoli and subsequently reused in the floor as a tomb slab.

Room I holds a number of small 15th-C paintings, largely from the Franchetti Collection, which trace the development of Venetian painting from the late Gothic period (represented by the *Madonna and Child*, by Giambono) to the beginning of the High Renaissance (Madonnas by the School of **Alvise Vivarini** and the early 16th-C Venetian school).

Room II, which has a 16th-C coffered ceiling taken from the Palazzo Giustiniani Faccalon alla Fava, holds more Renaissance paintings and small bronzes, including several pieces *all'antica*—deliberately made in imitation of antique sculptures that had recently come to light.

Room III displays small Venetian Mannerist bronzes of the 16th C, showing the characteristic love of the convoluted human form. On the walls are 16th-C paintings, notably **Giovanni Agostino da Lodi**'s *Pietà*.

Room VII holds Venetian paintings and sculptures of the High Renaissance, a series of Flemish tapestries, and one of **Anthony van Dyck**'s finest portraits, the *Portrait of Marcello Durazzo*. **Titian**'s *Venus at the Mirror* (the right side of which has been cut back) was a subject so popular the artist painted it more than once (the original is thought to be the version in the National Gallery in Washington) and numerous others copied it—from members of his workshop to the Flemish masters Pieter Paul Rubens and Lambert Sustris.

Also displayed are portrait busts by **Alessandro Vittoria**, the leading Venetian Mannerist, in which classical form is coupled with a profoundly critical insight into the individual character of the sitter. The bust of *Procuratore Marino Grimani*, in gilt terracotta, is particularly interesting for its technique and for its depth of psychological penetration.

SECOND FLOOR

PORTEGO

The second-floor portego displays a series of frescoes detached
from Venetian churches and public buildings and brought here for
safekeeping. On the end wall of the portego are the badly
weathered frescoes painted by Titian for the Fondaco dei Tedeschi,
once clearly visible to all traffic up and down Venice's main
thoroughfare, the Grand Canal.

The display cases hold terracotta sculptural maquettes, notably
two studies by **Gian Lorenzo Bernini** for the famous Fountain of
the Four Rivers in Piazza Navona in Rome. There are also two
beautiful view paintings by **Francesco Guardi**: *The Piazzetta Looking
Towards San Giorgio* and *The Molo Looking Towards the Church of the
Salute*.

Rooms VIII and IX display part of the museum's extensive holdings
of ceramics.

FLEMISH PAINTING

Room XI-XIII These rooms are devoted to German and Flemish
painters of the 15th and 16th centuries. Among the more beautiful
works in *Room XI* are **Daniel Hopfer**'s *St Jerome Kneeling Before the
Cross* and the small painting of the *Crucifixion* by **Jan van Eyck**,
displayed on an easel. *Room XII*, with a beautiful coffered ceiling
from the Casa De' Stefani in Verona, is hung with 17th-C Flemish
and Dutch landscapes and still lifes. The Arcadian vision of rural
life in vogue at the time is particularly evident in *View of a Riverside
Village* by Lodovico Toeput (called **Pozzoserrato**). The case by the
windows holds a beautifully executed *Sleeping Woman* by **Gabriel
Metsu**.

1

C.le d. Muti

Corte Vecchia
C. dei Trevisan
Fond. dell'Abbazia
C. Larga Lezze
Misericordia

A

Fond. della
Misericordia Fond. dell'Abbazia

Fond.
dramin
Fond. Forner
Fond. Trapolin
chiesa
Fond. Forner
C.

Noal
C. di Chiesa
Salamon
C. d. Stua
Fond. S. Felice
C. Larga
Dogal
C. Zotti
C. Pistor
Campo
S. Felice
C. Pensieri
C. Caotorta
C. delle Vele

B

Ca d'Oro
Galleria
Franchetti

Grand

Fondamenta
della Riva dell'Olio
Campiello
Ca d'Oro

Campo
Sta. Fosca
Strada
Nuova

Pescheria

C

C. Larga Beccarie
Campo
Beccarie
Ruga d. Spezieri
Calle Cristo
Calle Forno
C. d. Duca
Calle d'Oca
C. Pristi
Fabbriche
Nuove
C. della
Pescaria
C. Prima
C. Donzella
Calle S. Mattio
Ruga d. Oresi
Fabbriche
Vecchie
Erberia
Campo
S. Giacomo
Campo
Rialto Nuovo

Sotop. del
Cristi
del
Botteri
C. Aspri
Sansoni
C. del Sole
C. Donzella
Campo
Rialto Nuovo
Calle detta Madonna
Calle dei Cinque
Ruga
Ruga Vecchia
C. d'Orefici
Ruga
Calle S. Matio
Calle del
Paradiso
Calle dello Scaleter
Rio Terrà
124
Calle della
Rialto
del
Vin
Rialto
Campo
S. Silvestro
S. Silvestro
Fond.
otera

2

S. Caterina
C. Masena

Calle
lunga
Calle
della
Racchetta
Fond. S. Caterina
Corte
Squero
Vecchio
Fond. S. Andrea

Campo
S. Antonio

Fond. Foscarini
C. d. Cadene
C. d. Legnami
C. s. Botteri
C. Crociferi

Campo
S. Antonio
Fond. Zen
C.po
dei Gesuiti

C. d. Erbe
Calle Albanesi
Ruga Due Pozzi
C. Corrente
Rio Terrà
dei Franceschi
Calle Vele
Calle
Bembo
Calle Verde
Calle Forno
C. d. Tagliapietra
Rio
Terrà
SS. Apostoli
Sal. d. Pistor
C.
Proverbi
Rio Terrà
C.po dei
S.S. Apostoli
Campo
Ruga Vele
Ramo Albanesi

Sartori
Fond.
d. Sartori
Salizada
Scrimam
Fond
C. Posta
Ruga
Barba
C. d. Forno
C.llo
d. Cason
Rio Terrà
SS. Apostoli
Rio Terrà
Barba
C. d. Posta
C. d. Traghetto
Canal
Salizz.
San Canciano
Salizz. Seriman

3

Fondamenta

I Gesuiti

Oratorio dei
Crociferi

C. Volti
C. Venier
C.llo
d. Pietà
C. Remer
Frutarol
C. d. Forno
Calle Traghetto
Comello
Campo
S. Maria
Nuova
Santa Maria
dei Miracoli
C. Castell
Campo
S. Marina
Campo
S. Maria
Nova

Rio Terrà
dei Franceschi
San Giovanni
Crisostomo
C. Teatro
C. Asen
Salizz. S. Giov. Crisostomo
C. Dose
C. del Forno
C. Carminati
C. Martinengo
Campo
S. Lio
San Lio
C. Malvasia
C. Valle
C. delle Nave
C. Volto
C. Frava
Salizz.

Fondaco dei
Tedeschi
Rialto
Bridge
Campo
S. Bortolomio
Campo
S. Bortolomio
C. Bissa
Campo
Rialto
Riva di Ferro
Sal. Pio X
C. d. Zocco
Sal. Pio X
Galeazza
C. Stan

CANNAREGIO

in the area

THE SOUTHEAST END OF CANNAREGIO

I Gesuiti The church of Venice's Jesuit community is a rich and grand early 18th-C edifice with a lively Baroque façade based on Roman models. Nothing, however, quite prepares you for the effect of the interior. Like so many Jesuit churches in Italy, it is elaborately decorated—but in this case with a quite extraordinary work of trompe l'oeil, imitation damask executed with virtuoso skill in green and white inlaid marble.

Over the first north altar is **Titian**'s *Martyrdom of St Lawrence*, and in the transept on this side is an *Assumption* by **Tintoretto**. If it strikes you as odd that the seat of such an important order should be located so far from the mainstream of city life, you have not yet begun to understand Venetian psychology: the Senate managed to keep the powerful Jesuits out of the city for a long time, and when the order finally was allowed to establish itself, it was kept as far from the centres of political and economic affairs as topography would allow. **Map p. 124, 3A**

Santa Maria dei Miracoli Santa Maria dei Miracoli, a lonely little church in the narrow Campo dei Miracoli, is perhaps the loveliest architectural achievement of the whole early Venetian Renaissance. Constructed between 1481 and 1489 to enshrine a miraculous image of the Virgin, it is covered with coloured marble panels whose ingeniously complex design makes the church appear larger than it really is, but still maintains an atmosphere of harmonious tranquillity. The church is the work of Pietro Lombardo, who was assisted here by his sons Antonio and Tullio. The interior has exquisite Lombardesque marblework and a delightful *Madonna*, over the high altar, by Nicolò di Pietro Paradisi. From the canal and neighbouring bridges, the church appears like an ornate jewel-case (it is, after all, a reliquary church). Much of its dramatic effect, too, depends upon the cramped space it occupies. From whichever way you arrive it is a pleasurable surprise in all its whimsical magnificence. **Map p. 124, 3C**

San Giovanni Crisostomo The pleasant red and white church of San Giovanni Crisostomo, a masterpiece of Venetian Renaissance architecture, almost fills its small campo. The interior preserves two important paintings—Giovanni Bellini's *St Jerome with St Christopher and St Augustine* (over the first south altar) and the high altarpiece of *St John*

Chrysostom and Six Saints by Sebastiano del Piombo. An extraordinarily powerful, classically serene marble relief of the *Crowning of the Virgin* (over the second north altar) is by Tullio Lombardo. **Map p. 124, 2C**

THE NORTHERN END OF CANNAREGIO

Sant'Alvise Originally a convent church, Sant'Alvise was commissioned in honour of St Louis of Toulouse by the Venetian noblewoman Antonia Venier in 1388, after the saint had appeared to her in a dream. The single-aisled interior still contains its 15th-C nuns' choir, which rests on columns and buttresses and leads directly from the church to the nearby convent—one of the earliest known examples of its type. The present form of the church is the result of a 17th-C renovation, and a more successful one, as the daring perspective of the ceiling frescoes painted then by Antonio Torri and Pietro Ricchi is still spectacularly effective. There are also three early works by Giambattista Tiepolo: *Christ Carrying the Cross*, *Crowning with Thorns* and *Flagellation* (1737-40). **Map 113, 1A**

Madonna dell'Orto Flanked by the old Scuola dei Mercanti, this monumental church stands in a piazza that still maintains its original paving of herringbone brick with Istrian stone divisions. Originally built in the 14th C and rebuilt in the 15th C, the church owes its name to a miraculous statue of the Virgin and Child that was found in a nearby garden (*orto*). The statue is now in the San Mauro chapel, and, in fact, the church is officially dedicated to St Christopher. This was the parish church of Tintoretto, who was buried in the chapel on the south side of the sanctuary in 1594. Inside are several of his works: the *Presentation of the Virgin in the Temple* at the end of the south aisle, the *Last Judgement and Worship of the Golden Calf* in the choir, and the *Vision of the Cross to St Peter* and *Beheading of St Paul* in the apse. The latter are hung around an *Annunciation* by Palma Giovane. Other noteworthy works in the church include the fine complex of paintings in the Contarini Chapel (fourth chapel in the north aisle), where you can see Cima da Conegliano's *St John the Baptist and Saints* (first altar on the right). **Map 113, 2-3A**

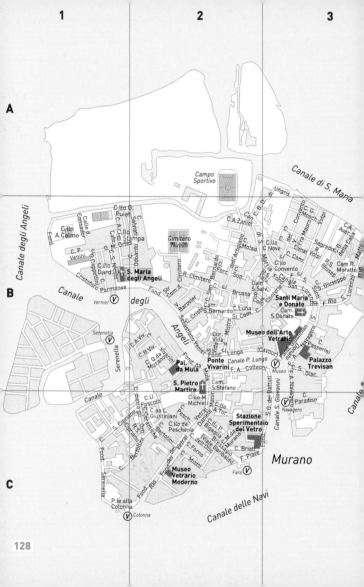

Museo dell'Arte Vetraria, Murano

OPEN The museum is open 10 am–4 pm, Tue-Mon, between Nov and March (ticket office 10 am–3 pm), and 10 am–5 pm, Tue-Mon, between April and Oct (ticket office 10 am–4 pm).

CLOSED Wed, 1/1, 1/5, 25/12

CHARGES Regular admission € 4.00. Children under 15, students 15-29 and EU seniors over 65, €2.50; children under 6, disabled people with escorts and other special categories free. Reduced admission with Museum Card and Museum Pass

GUIDED VISITS Audio guides; English-language guide available on request at 041 520 9038

DISABLED ACCESS Yes (ask at Reception)

SERVICES Cloakroom, museum shop

TELEPHONE 041 739 586

WEB www.museiciviciveneziani.it

MAIN ENTRANCE Fondamenta Giustinian 8, Murano

GETTING THERE Vaporetto 12 from Fondamenta Nuove. Remember to check schedules when you arrive on the islands, and to give yourself at least an hour to go to and from Venice.

HIGHLIGHTS

Roman glass **archaeological section**	Ground floor
Cristallino glass	First floor, 15th-C section
Barovier Cup	First floor, 19th-C section
Modern glass	First floor, 20th-C section

The Venetian glass factories were moved to the island of Murano as a safety measure in 1291 (because of the risk of fire), and the small, watery suburb has been synonymous with exquisite glass craftsmanship ever since. The Venetians had rediscovered the lost art of making clear 'crystal' glass in the 10th C, when merchants brought the secrets of the trade from the East, and they managed—by a combination of force and draconian legislation—to keep a proprietary hold on the secret until the 16th C. After a period of decline, glassmaking revived at the end of the 19th-C and is holding on today, partly as a tourist attraction—the many glass factories all welcome visitors to their workshops.

In the 16th-C Murano also became a favourite retreat of Venetian intellectuals, many of whom had splendid houses and luxuriant gardens. The small Grand Canal that runs between the town's shops and houses takes you to the Museo dell'Arte Vetraria, located in the 17th-C Palazzo Giustinian. The collection includes examples of antique glass from the 2nd C ad onwards, as well as fine examples of Venetian art from its heyday, all testifying to the enduring desire of artisans to solidify the shape of their imagination in the mysterious, changeable medium of glass.

THE BUILDING

Originally a patrician home in the Venetian Gothic style, in 1659 the palace became the residence of Marco Giustinian, Bishop of Torcello, under whose auspices it was rebuilt in its present form by Antonio Gaspari. It subsequently passed to the Venice Patriarchate, the city of Murano and, finally, the city of Venice. The

chandelier in the centre first-floor portego, by Giovanni Fuga and Lorenzo Santi, won a gold medal at the first Murano Glass Exposition in 1864.

THE COLLECTION

GROUND FLOOR

The glass in the *archaeological collection* comes mainly from Roman tombs in the eastern Adriatic, and includes funerary urns dating from the 1st and 2nd C AD. The exceptional quality and unexpected beauty and colour of Roman glassware at that time are demonstrated by the variety of designs and techniques.

FIRST FLOOR

THE 15TH CENTURY This was when Venetian craftsmen began to view blown glass as a means of artistic expression, just when the Islamic glass industry entered its decline. The invention of transparent glass, called *cristallino* on account of its clarity, was attributed to Angelo Barovier (1405-60), one of a dynasty of glass blowers whose fame continued over the following centuries. Decorative motifs at first were generally limited to bands of gilt or enamelled dots in a rosette pattern on the edges of the piece or grouped in tight semicircles (*embrici*).

Later on, the transparent glass produced in Venice was decorated in coloured fusible enamels, depicting allegorical triumphs, flowers, fruit and mythical figures inspired by paintings and engravings. The design of the glass pieces was based on those of the gold and silver vases in vogue at that time.

THE 16TH CENTURY An alternative to colourless crystalline glass emerged in the 16th C with the invention of an opaque white glass known as *lattimo*. It was sometimes enamelled, but more frequently made into long, thin canes that were incorporated into clear glass. Hence was born filigree glass, one of the more unusual kinds of glass to be produced by Renaissance glassmakers.

In the second quarter of the century, artisans began etching surfaces with a flint or diamond point to make flowers and animals so delicate that the glass appears to be trimmed with lace. Another new technique, *vetro ghiaccio*, involved creating a rough, cracked surface that was translucent but not transparent, giving the glass a frosted appearance. In some cases paint was applied to the finished glass piece and subjects were often drawn from paintings by celebrated artists. Towards the end of the century, feather-shaped decorations were obtained by 'combing' the *lattimo* threads into festoons, and with this burst of creativity, the fame of Murano glass spread throughout Europe.

THE 17TH CENTURY This was the century of glass *à la façon de Venise*, made abroad by local craftsmen in imitation of Venetian glass or, more frequently, by emigrant Murano glassmakers working all over Europe. In order to satisfy local taste, they accentuated the fanciful decorative motifs of the past with coloured glass. Nevertheless, the first signs of a decline in Venetian glass making became evident in the last quarter of the century as Bohemian glass—tougher and heavier than its Venetian counterpart and more suitable for deep engraving—became increasingly popular. The final humiliation came in the closing years of the century, as Venice began to imitate the engraving on Bohemian glass.

THE 18TH CENTURY At the beginning of the 18th C, craftsmen began producing glass that had the same chemical composition as Bohemian glass, and with the new technique of wheel engraving, decorative motifs from Bohemia employed with typically Venetian imaginative flourish resulted in a new kind of product called 'Bohemia-style' glassware.

Chiocche chandeliers decorated with festoons, flowers and leaves and Murano's famous coloured glass mirrors made their appearance at this time, as did the complex centrepieces called *deseri*, whose designs were often inspired by architecture, mythology, theatre scenes, festivities or games. Opaque white *lattimo* glass imitating porcelain also became widely popular.

The 18th-C glassmakers also produced glass imitations of precious stones and revived the 15th- and 16th-C tradition of decorating blown glass with colourful enamels.

THE 19TH CENTURY Napoleon's conquest of the Republic of Venice in 1797 was the beginning of a long series of political upheavals that exasperated the troubles of a glass industry already in decline. But when the Veneto region joined the newly established Kingdom of Italy in 1866, the revival of the Murano glass industry became possible. Blown glass was again popular abroad, especially in London, while some workshops began making imitations of Roman mosaic glass. Murano craftsmen were also attracted by early Christian gold-leaf glass, which they skilfully copied and exhibited at the Paris World's Fair in 1878. They were also inspired by enamelled glass, especially the **Barovier Cup**, which is still displayed in the museum. An effort was made to imitate the shape and appearance of antique pottery, giving rise to *corinto* glass, characterized by cracked gold, silver or green opaque paste on a dark background. Corinto, as well as pre-Roman style *fenici* glass and figurative *cameo* glass, were all supplanted by the Art Nouveau spirit towards the end of the century.

THE 20TH CENTURY Glassmaking in Murano continued along traditional lines at the beginning of the 20th C, but the more innovative creations of this period share the Art Nouveau interest in animal and floral designs. After World War I, Murano craftsmen began to work closely with internationally known painters and sculptors—a custom that has endured to the present day, the proof of which you can see in the galleries and shops of Venice.

SANTI MARIA E DONATO

Murano's main architectural monument is Santi Maria e Donato, a splendid example of the Veneto-Byzantine style, founded in the 7th C but rebuilt in the 12th C. It was originally dedicated to the Virgin Mary, but St Donato's name was added when his relics were brought here from Cephalonia, in Greece, together with the bones of a dragon he supposedly slew (four of which, to rebut sceptics, hang behind the altar). The church is known above all for its magnificent and beautifully restored Romanesque mosaic pavement (1141), but the capitals of the columns, the Byzantine mosaic of the Virgin in the apse and the colourful wooden altarpiece by Paolo Veneziano in the north aisle are also beautiful.

Torcello

Piazza di
Torcello

**Cathedral of
Santa Maria
Assunta**

Canale *di* *Torce*

Fond. del Borgognoni

Canale

Fond.

Torcello ⓥ

di

Borgognoni

Antonio

Sant'

Canale

Mazzorbo ⓥ

Fond. di Santa Caterina

Cimitero

Strada

del

Canale *di* *Burano*

ⓥ *Burano*

Fond. del

Burano

Sequeri

Burano

St. di Corte Comare

St. S. Mauro

C. Scarp

Sinistra

*C.dell'
Acqua*

*C.
Chibecchini*

C. Gen

C.Tfen.

V.di A. Marcell

F.S. Salad

C. Mauro

C. Assunti

Prepiero Capece

F.S.Chiesa

*V.
Principe*

*Cor.del
Pistor*

*C.llo
S.Vito*

C.
Boccanetto

C.
Scublette

*Corte
Comare*

Fond. Cao Molina

C. di Battello

Mastelli

C. Pittori

V. S. Mauro

C. Daffan

C. Gen

C. Pont.

F. Pont.

C. Cavalti

*V. di
Vigna*

C.Piovanello

C. Basadonna

*Cor.
Tonda*

Fond. S.Mauro

C.Pizzo

C. Ca Zane

C. Broetto

C.Fornani

C.Battelleto

C.Belladonna

C.Gobbi

C.Strullio

C.Matteotti

C.Tibaldon

C.Caltenti

Fond.

*Museo del
Merletto*

Piazza
B. Galuppi

Fond.
Terranova

C.Pellegrini

Mazzorbo

Cappuccine

Rio T. d.Pozzo

San Martino

134

Cathedral of Santa Maria Assunta, Torcello

OPEN	The cathedral is open 10 am–5 pm every day, and the museum is open 10 am–5 pm, Tue–Sun.
CLOSED	*Museum* Mon, 1/1, 1/5, 25/12
CHARGES	For the cathedral €3/€2. For the cathedral, museum and campanile €6 / €
GUIDED VISITS	Audio guides; English-language guide available on request at 041 520 9038
DISABLED ACCESS	Partial (there are steps)
SERVICES	Bookshop
TELEPHONE	*Cathedral* 041 270 2464 *Museum* 041 730 761
GETTING THERE	Vaporetto 12 or 14 from Fondamenta Nuove. Remember to check schedules when you arrive on the islands, and to give yourself at least an hour to go to and from Venice.

HIGHLIGHTS

Architecture of the 11th–15th centuries	Exterior and interior
Mosaics	Interior

The tiny island of Torcello was settled long before the main islands of the lagoon which we call Venice today. It was sought in desperation as a safe haven by refugees driven from the mainland city of Altinum, in the wake of fierce and repeated Lombard invasions. At least the shifting mudbanks and tidal channels of the lagoon gave this anonymous mud-bank some sort of protection.

Torcello subsequently grew and flourished between the 7th and the 13th centuries, when it may have had as many as 20,000 inhabitants. But rivalry with Venice and chronic malaria eroded its prestige and decimated its population. Now it is little more than a small group of houses in a lonely part of the lagoon, huddled in the shadow of a singular and impressive churche.

A visit to Torcello is a journey back in time, and it should be embarked upon in a spirit of tranquillity and leisure. Going at times that avoid the midday tours you will encounter an unforgettable atmosphere and often a magical light. The view from its tall campanile enraptured Ruskin and, in good light conditions, can do the same for visitors today.

The great **Cathedral of Santa Maria Assunta** is a ten-minute walk from the landing stage, down a lonely canal and past a few houses. Founded in 639, it was rebuilt in 864 and again in 1008. Before it stand the remains of the baptistery (the earliest element of the complex), and beside it is the tall detached campanile, a landmark of the lagoon.

The peaceful and chastely beautiful interior is among the most serene achievements of Christian religious architecture. Eighteen Greek marble columns with finely carved capitals separate the aisles and nave, and a superb 11th-C mosaic pavement covers the floor. Four elaborately carved screens, of Byzantine inspiration, mark the entrance to the sanctuary, with 15th-C paintings of the Virgin and Apostles above. The relics of St Heliodorus are preserved in a Roman sarcophagus beneath the 7th-C high altar, reminding us that this was once primarily a place of pilgrimage. The saint, who lived and died in the 4th C, was the first bishop of Altinum—the ancient inland town that existed before Venice—and a friend of St Jerome's. Set into the wall north of the altar is an inscription considered the oldest 'document' of Venetian history, an inscription commemorating the foundation of the church in 639.

The most striking feature of the church, however, is the important cycle of mosaics, completed before those in San Marco. The *Virgin and Child with Apostles* in the apse is one of the most splendid and important images of Byzantine art and the rival of any icon of that time. Made most likely by craftsmen from Constantinople, it represents a break with traditional iconography, usurping the position of Christ Pantocrator. Against its unearthly gold background, the figure of Mary is elegantly elongated and sublimely solitary.

The west wall of the church holds a vast mosaic of the *Last Judgement*, poorly restored in the 19th C when many areas were removed and replaced by copies. The most intact sections are those depicting the realm of hell and the seven deadly sins, and the mosaics are extremely powerful in the way they show the tremendous energy of the angels as they drive the Proud (bishops, cardinals, princes, colourful infidels and all …) into hellfire, the smoky burst of flame that envelops the lustful, the chill bodies of the greedy depicted engulfed by darkness, the sinister pallor that throws into relief the writhing serpents emerging from the eyes of the envious.

The Palazzo del Consiglio, across the lawn, now houses the MUSEO DELL'ESTUARIO DI TORCELLO, which contains an interesting collection of objects tracing the history of the island. It includes some objects from the cathedral—fragments of 12th-C mosaics and all that remains of the 13th-C silver-gilt altar frontal—as well as archaeological finds and a number of paintings from demolished churches in the area.

BURANO

Map p. 134 Burano, about an hour away from Venice, is a charming little fishing village full of brilliantly coloured houses which transfigure the hazy lagoon air. It is a delightful place just to wander. The parish church, with its alarmingly canted bell tower is charming to visit: it contains a few notable paintings, by Girolamo da Santacroce, Giambattista Tiepolo and Giovanni Mansueti. In past centuries the island was a favourite haunt of painters, who came for the light on the water, the walls and the picturesque *merlettaie*, or lace-makers. Lace, in fact, has been a mainstay of the island's economy since the early 16th C. If you plan to buy some, be sure to get the genuine variety, which you'll learn to recognize in the lace museum at the **Scuola di Merlietti** (open 10 am–5 pm, Wed–Mon, between April and Oct, and 10 am–4 pm on the same days between Nov and March; 041 730 034).

Before leaving Burano stroll over to its small sister island, **Mazzorbo**, whose pretty little canal is lined with fishing-nets spread out to dry in the sun. Here, too, is some of the best contemporary architecture in Venice: G. De Carlo's 1986 housing project fully respects local vernacular forms and colours.

eat

IN VENICE
RESTAURANTS

€ **Al Ponte** Cannaregio 6378, Ponte del Cavallo. 041 528 6157. This pretty little osteria is known for its straightforward, decent wines and delicious warm and cold meat dishes. Look for red shutters and one half-curtained window; inside are white walls crowded with slates and pictures. **Map p. 124, 3A**

La Cantina Cannaregio, 3688 Campo San Felice. Whether you sit inside or out, La Cantina is charming. It's dark and cozy inside, with candlelight gleaming off dark wood, while the outside tables let you watch the bustle of the Strada Nouva. The bruschette are numerous and excellent, the crostini are unforgettable, and everyone is friendly. Closed Sun. **Map p. 113, 3C**

La Perla Cannaregio 4615, Rio Terrà dei Franceschi. 041 528 5175. Probably the best pizzeria in town, La Perla is an absolutely basic restaurant. There are no frills, but there are a lot of tables to take care of a busy and faithful clientele. The pizzas range from the simple to the fanciful, but all are good value for money. If someone in your party isn't fond of pizza, there are also delicious full meals. Closed Sun and in Aug. **Map p. 124, 2B**

€€ **Boccadoro** Cannaregio 5405A, Campiello Widman. 041 521 1021. Creative cuisine by the former chef of Al Covo—from tasty pasta dishes to the freshest fish in Adriatic Italy. The small restaurant is just off the large, open campo at the church of Santa Maria dei Miracoli, and its simple elegance has made it a definite favourite with locals. Closed Mon. **Map p. 124, 3B**

Al Fontego dei Pescatori Cannaregio 3711, Sottoportego del Tagliapiera. 041 520 0538. Modern décor and seasonally changing menus based on fresh fish and vegetables are what characterises this restaurant. Surprisingly open and sunny. **Map p. 124, 2B**

Fiaschetteria Toscana Cannaregio 5719, San Giovanni Crisostomo. 041 528 5281. This should be a place on your list for truly delicious cuisine, both Tuscan and Venetian. The restaurant, run by the Busatto family, also has a list of around 500 excellent wines and pleasant outside seating in summer, and is not far from the bustling Rialto. Closed Tue and July–Aug. **Map p. 124, 2C**

Mirai Cannaregio 227, Rio Terrà Lista di Spagna. 041 220 6517. What's a famous cuisine whose use of seafood is particularly admired? Why, Japanese, of course. Mirai serves excellent Japanese food, from fresh sushi and sashimi to light, delicate tempura—all in a refreshingly modern atmosphere that gives you a break from antiquity. Closed Mon and in Jan. **Map p. 112, 2C**

Il Sole sulla Vecia Cavana Cannaregio 4624, Rio Terrà dei Santi Apostoli. 041 528 7106. Another newcomer to the neighbourhood. Restaurateur Stefano Monti has run more than one successful restaurant and knows how to please his guests with a relaxed, elegant atmosphere and always fresh ingredients. Closed Mon, Tues evening and in Jan and Aug. **Map p. 124, 2B**

Vini da Gigio Cannaregio 3628A, Fondamenta San Felice. 041 528 5140. Just off the bustling Strada Nuova is Vini da Gigio, is one of the best values in town, with delicious Venetian cooking for the happy few who find a table. Simple, intimate and friendly, the restaurant is run by the dedicated Lazzari family in old-style manner. Despite the name, it's not a wine bar, but the wine selection is still very good. Closed Mon and all of Jan-Feb and Aug-Sept. **Map p. 113, 3B**

WINE BARS

€ **Alla Frasca** Cannaregio 5176, Campiello della Carità. A time-honoured establishment in historic quarters (Titian stored his paints and canvas here) pleasantly situated in an out-of-the-way part of town. **Map p. 124, 3B**

Anice Stellato Cannaregio 3272, Fondamenta de la Sensa. 041 720744. Good ambience and delicious, reasonably priced food make this osteria a favourite of Venetians; closed Sun and late July–early Aug. **Map p. 113, 1A**

Cantina Vecia Carbonera Cannaregio 2329, Ponte Sant'Antonio. Great Italian and regional wines, delicious snacks and live music on Sunday, across from the chiesa della Maddalena; closed Mon, Sat–Sun evenings, and in Aug. **Map p. 112, 3B**

Dalla Marisa Cannaregio 652B, Fondamenta San Giobbe. 041 720211. Marisa is the daughter of a butcher: book ahead to get a jump on the locals (read, gondolieri) who swarm to this popular little place for her meat-based cooking; closed Sun and Wed evenings, 25/12 and in Aug. **Map p. 112, 1B**

La Colombina Cannaregio 1828, Campiello del Pegolotto. 041 275 0622. Good wine and simple but delicious food in a little square near the Strada Nova; closed Tues and Jan. **Map p. 113, 1B**

CAFÉS

€ **Bari ai Miracoli** Cannaregio 6066A, Campo San Felice. Tucked away in a little campo behind the church of Santa Maria dei Miracoli, serving sandwiches and pastries outside in summer, or, in winter, in cosy booths inside. **Map p. 113, 3C**

Boscolo Cannaregio 1818, Campiello de l'Anconeta. Busy pasticceria offering a superb selection of Venetian pastries. **Map p. 113, 1B**

ON THE ISLANDS

€ **Antica Trattoria alla Maddalena** Mazzorbo 7C. 041 730151. Forty minutes to an hour by boat from Venice is the island of Mazzorbo, which huddles against the bigger Burano. Alla Maddalena is a restaurant to go for old-fashioned lagoon food—try the *selvadego de vale* (wild fowl) and *castraure* (baby artichokes). Everything is made locally, including the famous Burano *bussolái*, a sweet but plain flour biscuit formed into a ring, made to eat with your wine. Closed Thur and Dec–Jan. **Map p. 134**

€€ **Al Gatto Nero Burano** Fundamenta della Giudecca 88. 041 730120. In picturesque surroundings near the fish market, this friendly trattoria serves delicious dishes in the best Venetian tradition. It's a large restaurant (a change from the aged and smoke-darkened wood of many of Venice's restaurants), so it's popular with groups, and can be full. Closed Mon and, Jan and Nov. **Map p. 134**

Busa alla Torre Murano, Campo Santo Stefano 3, 041 739 662. A good place to have lunch on Murano, with tables in a pretty little square in summer. The food is delicious, no-frills Venetian cooking year round, including *moeche*, a small, soft-shelled crab. Bear in mind that it's only a lunch place, however, and is closed evenings. **Map p. 128, 2B**

€€€**Locanda Cipriani** Torcello, Piazza S. Fosca 29. 041 730 150. This rustic, yet upscale restaurant attached to the locanda is part of Venice's Cipriani empire. Giancarlo Cipriani, the founder of Harry's Bar, set up the hotel in the 1930s. The restaurant is known for dishes like *insalatina novella con scampi al sesamo, tagliatelle nere con ragout di vongole e capesante, sorpresa di mare in crosta* and *semifreddo alla Grappa di Picolit.* Closed Tue and Nov–Mar. **Map p. 134**

shop

ACCESSORIES

Frutta e Verdura Cannaregio 4451, Campo Santi Apostoli. The 'fruits and vegetables' here aren't the edible type, but are inspirations for colour, texture and design. The label turns silk, velour, linen and silk/wool blends into beautiful bags, scarves and other objects of tactile desire—run your fingers lightly over the velvet and you'll see what we mean. **Map p. 124, 2B**

BOOKS

Laboratorio Blu Cannaregio 1224, Campo del Ghetto Vecchio. A playground and bookshop for the under-15 set, this shop has more

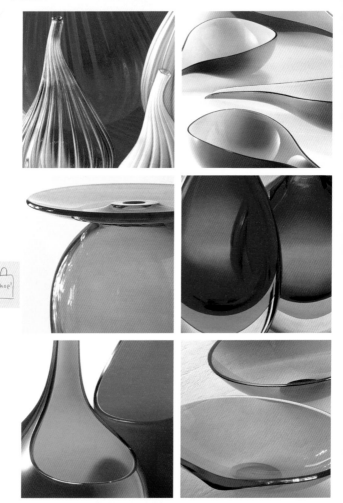

shop!

than children's books, it has readings and mini-courses in fine arts and theatre. Most things are in Italian, but there are also books in English. **Map p. 112, 3B**

GLASS

What to look for in Murano glass? The answer is as various as the styles Murano glassmasters have used through history. A visit to the Museo dell' Arte Vetraria (see p. 129) is a good place to start for a look at the traditional glassmaking methods, which range from clear cristallino glass to white lattimo and up to brilliant polychrome chalcedony. Moving forward, contemporary innovation has seen glassmakers pairing up with young and established artists to create sleek, modern designs as well as elegant, design-conscious stemware and vases. It's well worth it to take time to visit a workshop's furnace on your way to the showroom, as part of the fascination of glassmaking is to see a flowing, molten globule of glass stretched and formed into an elegant bubble, then harden into its final, crystalline form.

Barovier & Toso Murano Fondamenta Vetrai 28. Barovier is the most famous name in Murano glass, and the family has an impressive pedigree: Angelo Barovier (1405-1460) is the father of clear, or cristallino, glass. Now the workshop makes fabulous traditional glass but is especially known for contemporary glass, though created by a company established in 1295. **Map p. 128, 2C**

Bisanzio Murano, Calle Paradiso 22. This firm, established in 1816, offers traditional and contemporary glass vases, plates, sculptures, chandeliers and other designs. Like many workshops, it allows visitors to watch the craftsmen at work. **Map p. 128, 3C**

C.A.M. Murano, Piazzale alla Colonna 1. A good place for mirrors and objets d'art, or for demonstrations of traditional chandelier-making techniques offered in the adjoining workshop. **Map p. 128, 1C**

Cesare Toffolo Murano, Bressagio 8A and Fondamenta Manin 75. Cesare Toffolo is another glass master from a glass family—at fifteen he learned the art from his father, who had learned from

Opposite: Glass from the Salviati Collection

Cesare's grandfather. Toffolo is renowned as a technical innovator, and has travelled around the world as an instructor. He is also a founder of the Centro Studio Vetro, a not-for-profit organisation that promotes education and cultural activities concerning all aspects of the art of glassmaking. **Map p. 128, 2B**

Gambaro & Poggi Murano, Calle Vivarini 6. Mario Gambaro and Bruno Poggi both grew up on the beautiful island of Murano, steeped in the history of glassmaking. After working through their apprenticeships at prestigious workshops, they branched out on their own in 1974. Now their workshop is one of the more prolific and interesting glass workshops in Murano. **Map p. 128, 2B**

Nason & Moretti Murano, Fondamenta Serenella 12. This venerable factory specialises in beautifully decorative and elegant stemware. Their collections are divided by period, with the simplicity of Romantic leading to the gilt-edged Gothic and the fripperies of Baroque. There's also a Contemporary line, with twirled bands of colour. **Map p. 128, 1C**

Salviati Murano, Fondamenta Radi 16. The story of Salviati is in many ways the story of modern Venetian glassmaking. In the mid-19th C, Venice glass was eclipsed by Bohemian work and Murano workshops were in decline. Lawyer Antonio Salviati's workshop attracted the masters, and new techniques taught at his school are credited with reviving the art—that, and Salviati's unerring business sense. Now the workshop produces exquisite classic modern and contemporary glass, including jewellery. **Map 128, 3B**

Seguso Murano, Fondamenta Serenella 3. When poet Gabriele d'Annunzio mentions a glass master in his masterpiece Fuoco, it's one of the Seguso family—and the firm's chandeliers are still a top choice of buyers from around the world. The Segusos began their workshop six hundred years ago, but their more recent fame stems from Archimede Seguso's master work in the 1950s. The company is still a family business, with Archimede's son Giampaolo now heading the firm and a new generation involved in design and marketing. **Map p. 128, 1C**

Venini Murano, Fondamenta Vetrai 47. Venini glass dates back to 1921, when Giacomo Cappellin and Paolo Venini founded a workshop. The spirit of innovation and modernity had great force at that time, and Venini made a break with traditional styles and focused on the avant-garde. Now many others have followed the sleek lines of Venini art glass, turning the once rebel into an established name. **Map p. 128, 2C**

CASTELLO, SAN GIORGIO & THE GIUDECCA

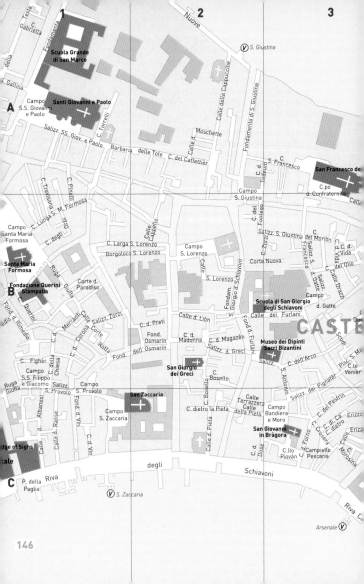

Grande

1 **2** **3**

A

Campo S. Daniele

Stretta

Calle Larga S. Pietro

Campo S. Pietro

San Pie

C. d. Terco

C. d. Campanile

C. S. Giovanni in Riello

Campo di Ruga

Calle Maraffoni

Fond. Quintavalle

C. Sporca

C. Riello

C. Salamón

C.po

Po

Fondamenta della Tana

Fond. Fornèr

C. Casparzoto

C. d. Bianco

C. Croclera

Calle S. Anna

Corte d. Coltrera

Calle S. Francesco di P.

C. Frizier

C. Loredan

C. Bassa

Fond. S. Gioacchino

Fondamenta S. Anna

Fondamenta

Corte Nuova

Calle dei Preti

B

C. Fur C. P.C.

Giuseppe Garibaldi

Corte Schiavoni

Sotto Calle di Pistòr

C. Pedrochi

Calle S. Domenico

Viale Garibaldi

Stretta Saresin

Calle dell'Angelo

C. Saresin

Corte Saresin

Rio Terrà dal Fornèr

C. Secco Marina

Ramo dei Nicoli

Calle delle Ancore

Calle delle Furlane

Calle da Lisina

Corte Pietro d. Cenere

Calle Catapán

Calle G. B. Tiepolo

Calle Correra

Corte Correra

Corte Magazen

Corte d. Solda

Marina

Calle Sabbioncella

Calle d. Prete

Corte Martin Novello

Secco

Fondamenta

S. Giuseppe

Corte d. Cristo

dei

Sette

Martiri

Campo S. Giuseppe

Rio Terrà S. Giuseppe

Paludo S. Antonio

Calle dentro il Giardino

Biennale

Giardini Ⓥ

Viale Giardini

Viale dei Giardini

Pubblici

V.le Trieste

Trento

Giardini Pubblici

C

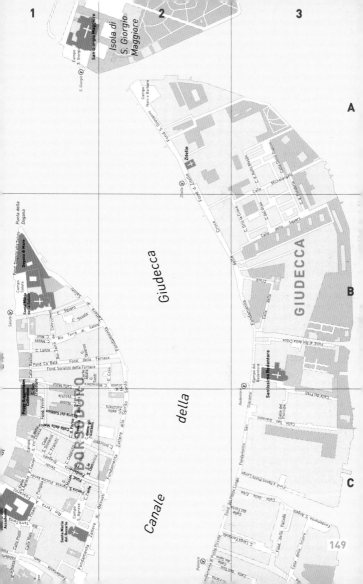

1 **2** **3**

A

B

C

Isola di
S. Giorgio
Maggiore

San Giorgio Maggiore

Campo S. Giorgio

S. Giorgio ⓥ

GIUDECCA

Zitelle

Fond. S. Giovanni

Zitelle ⓥ Fond.e Zitelle

Croce

Calle Michelangelo

Calle D. Dirà da Chiesa

Calle dello Squero

Calle Gràn

Calle di Croce

Calle Erizzo

Fond. al Rio della Croce

Fondamenta

Fondamenta

C. e. Ariàn Marsin

C. e. Ferràndo

Santissimo Redentore

Campo del Redentore

Fondamenta San Giacomo

Calle del Pistor

Calle dei Frati

Redentore ⓥ

Giudecca

Calle del Prencipe

Fond. S. Biagio Ponte Lungo

Fond. Rio del Ponte Lungo

Campo
Marte e Barbarie

Punta della
Dogana

Dogana di Mare

Dogana alla Salute

Fond. Dogana alla Salute

Santa Maria
della Salute

Salute ⓥ

Campo della Salute

C. Squero

C. Scuola

C. Meri

Rio Terra ai Saloni

Saloni

Fondamenta Zàttere ai Saloni

C. Mazzo

Rio Terra

C. Lanza

Fond. Ca' Balà

Fond. della Fornace

Fond. Soranzo detta Fornace

Calle del Basilio

Ramo Martini

C. Manisero

Calle Mora

Scala del Santo

Sant...

DORSODURO

Peggy Guggenheim Collection

Fond. Venier

Calle Venier

Fondamenta Nuova

Calle del Bastion

F. S. Cristoforo

Corte...

Campazzo

Rio Terra...

Gesuàti

Zàttere allo Spirito Santo

Calle dello Spirito Santo

Fondamenta Zàttere allo Spirito Santo

Accademia

Rio Terra A. Foscarini

Calle Nova

Foscarini

C. delle Mende

Fond. Ospedaletto

Calle delle Mende

P. Pignater

Calle d. Pistor

Vìdal

C. Toletta

Fondamenta Rio...

Calle Querini

S. Agnese

Fond. S. Agnese

S. Gerardo Sagredo

Calle S. Gerardo

S. Vìo

Piscina Forner

Campo

Santa Maria
del Rosario

Fondamenta Zàttere ai Gesuàti

Fond. Nani

C. Chiesa

Canale

Giudecca

della

149

Looking at the crowded quay that stretches eastwards from the Palazzo Ducale to the Giardini di Castello, you'd never guess that one of the quieter and more relaxed areas of Venice lies just behind San Marco. If you leave the waterfront, just a few paces inland you find some of the more delightful and magnificent achievements of Venetian art and architecture.

And across from San Marco and Dorsoduro are the islands of San Giorgio and the long, narrow Giudecca, each of which has a magnificent church by Palladio, famous for the purity and subtlety of his architecture. The Giudecca is also a wonderful place just to wander for atmosphere alone, as it's one of the only spots in Venice that tourists seem to have forgotten.

Fondazione Querini Stampalia

OPEN	The Fondazione is open 10 am–6 pm Tue-Thur and Sun, and 10 am–10 pm Fri and Sat.
CLOSED	Mon
CHARGES	Regular admission €6.00; students, seniors over 60, Museum Card and Rolling Venice Card holders €4.00. Admission is free for the disabled and their escorts and various other categories.
GUIDED VISITS	Audio guides; English-language guide available on request at 041 520 9038
DISABLED ACCESS	Partial

SERVICES	Café, cloakroom, museum shop
TELEPHONE	041 271 1411
WEB	www.querinistampalia.it
MAIN ENTRANCE	Castello 4778, Campo Santa Maria Formosa
GETTING THERE	Vaporetto 1 or 52 to San Zaccaria stop

HIGHLIGHTS

18th-C architecture and decor	Exterior and interior
20th-C architecture by Carlo Scarpa and Mario Botta	Interior and garden
Giambattista Tiepolo, *Portrait of the Procurator Dolfin* **Pietro Longhi's** *genre scenes*	Museum, 2nd floor

The Fondazione Querini Stampalia is an important library and picture gallery housed in a palace of 1528. The building was renovated in the 1960s to a design by Carlo Scarpa, the most prominent Italian architect of the time (who also designed the garden), and again in the 1990s by Swiss architect Mario Botta.

The Museo Querini Stampalia is situated on the second floor. The collection, which was completely rearranged in 1995–96, reflects the personal taste of the founder, Count Giovanni Querini, and his interest in the social portraits, conversation pieces and rich furnishings of 18th-C Venice.

The Querini Stampaglia mounts changing exhibitions of contemporary art (the neon writing on the main façade is by the American Conceptual artist Joseph Kosuth) and the library is the most popular in Venice for scholars, with its manuscripts, incunabula, rare books and prints, including antique maps, assembled over seven centuries by the Querini Stampalia family.

The rooms are decorated in light pastel colours, with stuccoed ceilings, mirrors and boiserie; Murano chandeliers and tapestries; Meissen, Vezzi, Sèvres and Cozzi porcelain; sculptures by Orazio Marinali and Antonio Canova; and globes by

Willem Blaue and Gilles-Robert de' Vaugondy. Marble busts, a
fresco of *Dawn and Dusk* and a great coloured Murano glass
chandelier greet the visitor in the portego, still the entrance hall
of this sumptuous suite of apartments. The Stanza Nuziale has an
allegorical ceiling fresco by Jacopo Guarana representing *Zephyr
and Flora* and green lacquer furniture by Zuanne and Alvise
Querini. The dining room is set up as it would have appeared in
the late 18th C, with the famous Sèvres porcelain service
acquired in Paris, in 1795-96, by Alvise Querini, the last
ambassador of the Serenissima Repubblica to France.

THE COLLECTION

The museum preserves one of the more extensive art collections
in the city, with more than 400 paintings ranging in date from the
14th to the 19th centuries.

The lovely *Presentation of Jesus in the Temple* (c. 1460) by **Giovanni
Bellini** was attributed to Andrea Mantegna until the early-20th-C
American critic and connoisseur Bernard Berenson recognized it
as a work of Bellini. Mantegna had, in fact, painted a larger
version of the same composition around 1454, to celebrate his
marriage with Nicolosia Bellini, Giovanni's sister. But that painting
(now in Berlin) has an entirely different feeling, as well as
considerable stylistic differences. Some critics think the young
man on the right of the Presentation might be a self-portrait,
while the young woman on the left is thought to be Giovanni's
sister Nicolosia and the figure of Joseph, in the centre
background, his father Jacopo.

Lorenzo di Credi's tondo of the *Virgin and the Young Saint John
Adorning the Child* (c. 1480), traditionally ascribed to Bartolommeo
Montagna, was attributed to di Credi for the first time in a 19th-C
inventory. It shows a clear debt to Verrocchio, and it may be an
early work, made when the great Florentine sculptor was in
Venice. This is one of Lorenzo's purer, more rarefied paintings,
and its colour, lighting and composition recalling paintings of this
subject by Filippo Lippi and Botticelli.

Jacopo Palma il Vecchio's portraits of *Francesco Querini* and *Paola Priuli Querini* (1527-28) remind us that we are looking at a private, personal collection. It was customary in the 16th C for fiancés to exchange portraits as wedding gifts, and this set was painted for the union of Francesco di Zuanne di Nicolò Querini Stampalia and Paola Priuli di Zan Francesco in the spring of 1528. Unfortunately the artist died before completing the paintings, and the details are sketchily rendered. The naturalism of the portraits and their effort to probe the psychology of the subjects suggest Palma may have based his approach on examples of Titian's portraiture.

Among the 18th-C paintings is the pièce de resistance of the Querini Stampalia collection, **Giambattista Tiepolo**'s *Portrait of the Procurator Dolfin*, painted between 1750 and 1755. This kind of portrait was unusual for Tiepolo, as his imagination was attracted mainly by mythological or historical subjects. The sitter has been tentatively identified as Daniele Dolfin IV (1656–1723), a captain in the Venetian navy and Procurator of the Republic, for whom the young Tiepolo had painted a series of Roman generals. The cruel energy in the gloved hand and the sinisterly spectral white wig are perfectly in keeping with the prestige of such a position, and the daring perspective and the theatrically billowing draperies give the painting an expressive power so strong that it verges on caricature.

Also in the 18th-C collection are beautiful little genre scenes by **Pietro Longhi**, including *Il Ridotto* (1757-60), one of several variations on this theme painted by Longhi (see the front cover of this book). The young lady at the centre, in *bautta* (fancy dress) with a red flower pinned to her breast, has removed her mask, revealing her identity. The unabashedly forward masked gentleman at her side grasps a fold of her magnificent silk dress, and the action unfolds beneath the smug gaze of an unmasked gentleman in *bautta* seated in the left foreground, whose expression betrays licentious admiration for the lady's beauty. In the right-hand corner a dog, symbolizing fidelity, has curled up and gone to sleep. Behind the principal players another couple, beneath a painted depiction of Venus, appear in a more advanced stage of amorous intimacy. The scene is completed by two plebeian women (on the left) masked with the mysterious oval *moretta*, one carrying a basket with birds, the other wearing a pink headscarf called a *nizzoletto*. On the right a group of gamblers have dropped cards in their enthusiasm.

Santi Giovanni e Paolo

OPEN	The church is open 8 am–sunset every day.
CHARGES	€2.50
GUIDED VISITS	The Venetian Association of Certified Tour Guides (041 520 9038) offers guided tours in English and other languages to all city monuments.
DISABLED ACCESS	Yes
SERVICES	Bookshop
TELEPHONE	041 523 7510
MAIN ENTRANCE	Castello 4693
GETTING THERE	Vaporetto 1 to Rialto stop

HIGHLIGHTS

Andrea Verrocchio, *Colleoni Monument*	The square
Gothic architecture	The church
Pietro Lombardo, *Monument to Pietro Mocenigo*	Interior, west wall
Giovanni Bellini, *St Vincent Ferrer Flanked by Saints Christopher and Sebastian*	Interior, south aisle
Lorenzo Lotto, *St Anthony Giving Alms*	Interior, south transept
Bartolomeo Vivarini and Gerolamo Mocetto, *Window of Warrior Saints*	Interior, south transept

SANTI GIOVANNI E PAOLO

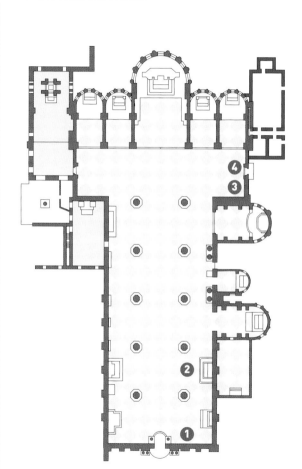

THE CAMPO

From a maze of tiny passageways you burst out into the impressive open space of the Campo Santi Giovanni e Paolo ('San Zanipolo' in Venetian dialect), which curves around the imposing Dominican church of Santi Giovanni e Paolo and the small marble façade of the Scuola di San Marco. The space is energized by the presence of the fine bronze equestrian monument to mercenary general Bartolommeo Colleoni, the last and grandest work of the Florentine sculptor **Andrea Verrocchio**, who was Leonardo da Vinci's teacher.

Verrocchio has masterfully created a horse which is strong and unruly, its veins swollen and muscles tense. Erect in the saddle, with his torso twisted against the movement of the horse's head, the general frowns down with fierce pride, in full command of his nervous charger.

The story of the statue is an amusing one. Colleoni, who had very successfully commanded the land forces of the Venetian Republic, died in 1475, leaving a considerable sum of money and reequesting a monument to his own glory. The legacy stipulated that the statue should be in the square of San Marco, but the authorities were constitutionally bound not to permit a self-glorifying monument to a single individual to be erected in the city's main public square. They obtained the legacy by putting the statue up in the square in front of the Scuola of San Marco—fulfilling, in a strictly literal sense, the terms of the will.

THE CHURCH

The surprisingly light and airy church of Santi Giovanni e Paolo is the second largest Gothic church in Venice and was begun in the mid-14th C and consecrated in 1430. It is a treasure house of sculpture and painting.

From the 15th C on, San Zanipolo was the traditional site for doges' funerals, and splendid Gothic and Renaissance monuments to 25 of the Republic's leaders line the walls. The most impressive of these is the *Monument to Pietro Mocenigo* [1]—

whose family occupies the entire west wall—by **Pietro Lombardo** (1476). Two paintings are of special note: **Giovanni Bellini**'s gentle triptych of *St Vincent Ferrer Flanked by Saints Christopher and Sebastian* **[2]** (near the Lombardo tomb, in the south aisle) and **Lorenzo Lotto**'s warm, sensitive *St Anthony Giving Alms* **[3]**, in the south wing of the transept. Here also is the last surviving example of the large painted glass windows that were a speciality of Murano glassmakers, the *Window of Warrior Saints* (1515) **[4]**.

SCUOLA GRANDE DI SAN MARCO

On the piazza's north side is the Scuola Grande di San Marco, now the city hospital. (Who could imagine a more beautiful building to be hospitalised in?) The palace, largely a work of the early Renaissance, has a splendid, coloured marble façade with sophisticated trompe l'oeil reliefs in which a marvellous sense of depth is obtained from a two-dimensional surface. From the ground floor hall you can enter the former Dominican convent of Santi Giovanni e Paolo, rebuilt by Baldassare Longhena in 1660–75 on a 13th-C plan around two cloisters and a courtyard.

San Giorgio and the Santissimo Redentore

Opposite Piazza San Marco and the Punta della Dogana are the islands of San Giorgio and the Giudecca. Conveniently reached by vaporetti that leave from the Castello quay known as the Riva degli Schiavoni, these two islands hold two of the highest architectural masterpieces of the Renaissance, Palladio's churches of San Giorgio Maggiore and the Santissimo Redentore.

OPEN	The churches are open every day 9.30 am–12.30 pm and 2.30–4.30 pm. In summer they stay open until 6 pm.
CHARGES	None, but the Fandazione Cini is only open by reservation at 041 5227 827.
GUIDED VISITS	The Venetian Association of Certified Tour Guides (041 520 9038) offers guided tours in English.
DISABLED ACCESS	Yes
TELEPHONE	*San Giorgio* 041 522 7827
MAIN ENTRANCE	*San Giorgio* Isola di San Giorgio Maggiore *Santissimo Redentore* Giudecca 195
GETTING THERE	Vaporetto 82 to San Giorgio stop or vaporetto 82, 41 or 42 to Redentore stop

HIGHLIGHTS

Architecture by Palladio	San Giorgio Maggiore, Santissimo Redentore
Architecture by Baldassare Longhena	San Giorgio Maggiore
Tintoretto, *Last Supper* and *Gathering of Manna*	San Giorgio Maggiore
Vittore Carpaccio, *St George and the Dragon*	San Giorgio Maggiore
Palma Giovane, *Deposition* Jacopo Tintoretto, *Ascension* Alvise Vivarini, *Madonna and Child with Angels* Paolo Veronese, *Baptism of Christ*	Santissimo Redentore

SAN GIORGIO MAGGIORE

The most striking building on the island is **Andrea Palladio**'s church of San Giorgio Maggiore, built between 1565 and 1580 over the remains of earlier churches dating back as far as the 8th C. The campanile is a later construction, built in 1792.

EXTERIOR

Palladio and his contemporaries were convinced that a harmony like that of music underlay the great buildings of the past, and that the secrets of that harmony could be unravelled by a careful study of mathematical proportions. You can see this belief at work on the façade of San Giorgio, where the triangle ideally formed by the lateral pediments reaches its apex at the base of the central pediment—an ingenious expedient that prepares the visitor, visually, for the aisled church within. It is Palladio's most complex church front design, and yet it strikes us with an apparently natural simplicity. It was only completed after his death.

INTERIOR

The interior has a remarkable sculptural quality based on the opposition between flat and rounded forms—walls, arches and vaults, engaged columns and giant pilasters—and decoration is almost totally eliminated. Its art treasures include two works by **Tintoretto**, the *Last Supper* and the *Gathering of Manna*, on the walls around the high altar (1594). The gift of manna to the Israelites in the wilderness provided the Old Testament parallel to the bread and wine of the Eucharist, and the paintings were designed to be most effective when seen by from the altar rail. Over the altar of the winter choir is a *St George and the Dragon* by Vittore Carpaccio.

The **campanile**, reached by a lift behind the main altar, is 60 m high and offers unsurpassed views of the city and the lagoon.

MONASTERY

The monastery of San Giorgio Maggiore is arranged around two cloisters. Palladio, in designing the magnificent and serene refectory, created one of the greatest and most calming spaces of Renaissance architecture. In the park the Teatro Verde does open-air theatre. The complex is generally only open to the public for temporary exhibitions and other special events.

Palladio's Santissimo Rendentore

SANTISSIMO REDENTORE

The church of the Redentore is one of the most venerated churches in Venice, and the centrepiece of one of the most deeply felt public celebrations (the Feast of the Redentore, on the third Sunday in July). Commissioned by the Senate to honour a vow taken during the terrible plague of 1575-77, the church was designed by **Palladio** in 1577 and completed after the architect's death by Antonio da Ponte. It is indisputably one of the great masterpieces of Renaissance architecture.

EXTERIOR

The overall scheme of the façade is regulated by a complicated system of proportions and superimposition of pure geometric shapes. It is a development and expansion of the church of San Francesco della Vigna (see p. 163), which Palladio had designed some ten years earlier, with pediments over the door and central bay and the end sections of a hidden pediment emerging on either side of the main block.

INTERIOR

From the door the church appears as a simple rectangular basilica with an apse, but as you approach the high altar, the curves of the dome and arms gradually reveal themselves, giving a wonderful sense of elation and expansion. Over the altars are paintings by 16th and 17th C painters, notably a *Deposition* by Palma Giovane and an *Ascension* by Jacopo Tintoretto and assistants. Over the Baroque high altar (which Palladio certainly didn't anticipate) is a crucifix between 16th-C bronze statues of *St Mark* and *St Francis* and in the sacristy are a *Madonna and Child with Angels* by Alvise Vivarini and a *Baptism of Christ* by Paolo Veronese.

in the area

IN CASTELLO

Campo Santa Maria Formosa From Piazza San Marco, take the Mercerie (beneath the clock tower) to the church of San Zulian, then Calle delle Bande right to Campo Santa Maria Formosa. This pleasant and lively square is like a wonderful Venetian stage-set: in fact it was formerly used for open-air theatre. It is surrounded by fine palaces.

The church of Santa Maria Formosa was built, according to tradition, in 639 following a miraculous apparition of the Virgin Mary. It preserves a *Madonna of Mercy* by Bartolomeo Vivarini, signed and dated 1473, and a polyptych with *St Barbara and Four Saints* by Palma Vecchio. St Barbara was the patron of the artillerymen who had their chapel in this church. In the church's Oratory is a *Madonna with Child* painted by Giandomenico Tiepolo. **Map p. 146, 1B**

San Giorgio dei Greci In a shady garden by the narrow Rio di Greci is San Giorgio dei Greci, a 16th-C church built to a design by Sante Lombardo for the Greek Orthodox community. This is the most important foreign church in Renaissance Venice, and has a magnificently decorated interior divided by a marble iconostasis with late Byzantine gold-ground paintings.

On the north, in the rooms of the former **Scuola dei Greci** (now the Istituto Ellenico), is the Museo dei Dipinti Sacri Bizantini (open 9 am–12.30 pm and 1.30 pm–4.30 pm Mon-Sat, and 10 am–5 pm Sun and holidays; 041 522 6581). The museum has some 80 Byzantine and post-Byzantine icons and liturgical objects. One of the highlights is a hieratic icon of *St Anastasius* by the 16th-C painter Michele Damaskinos, who is credited with having encouraged a young artist from Crete who was in Venice at the time—Domenikos Theotokopoulos—to absorb all he could from Tintoretto's work. Theotokopoulos then moved on to Spain, where he would establish a reputation under the name of El Greco. **Map p. 146, 2B**

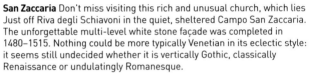

San Zaccaria Don't miss visiting this rich and unusual church, which lies Just off Riva degli Schiavoni in the quiet, sheltered Campo San Zaccaria. The unforgettable multi-level white stone façade was completed in 1480–1515. Nothing could be more typically Venetian in its eclectic style: it seems still undecided whether it is vertically Gothic, classically Renaissance or undulatingly Romanesque.

The radial chapels lit by tall windows are unique in Venice, and almost every space available is occupied by paintings, None, however, commands our attention as immediately as the heavenly vision and harmonious colours of Giovanni Bellini's *Madonna and Saints* on your left as you enter. It is signed and dated 1505, and was executed when the painter was in his seventies. It seems that a lifetime's meditation on how to catch the quintessence of the elusive Venetian light is brought to bear in this perfect and majestic altarpiece, which was to have such a great influence on later Venetian painting. **Map p. 146, 2C**

Scuola di San Giorgio degli Schiavoni The scuola (open 9.30 am–12.30 pm and 3.30 pm–6 pm Tues–Sat, 9.30 am–12.30 pm Sun and holidays; 041 522 8828) was built in the early 16th C by the Dalmatian confraternity, whose members were mainly merchants involved in trade with the East. The beautiful painting cycle on the walls of its ground floor walls is one of the artistic jewels of Venice and should not be missed. Executed by Vittore Carpaccio, who worked in Venice between 1490 and 1523, the richly fantastic scenes portray episodes from the lives of three protectors of Dalmatia, Saints George, Jerome and Tryphon, with great narrative clarity and charm. **Map p. 146, 2B**

San Giovanni in Bràgora This church has some masterpieces of Gothic and Renaissance painting, including numerous works by Alvise Vivarini: *Resurrected Christ, Madonna with Saints Andrew and John the Baptist, Praying Madonna and Child* and a panel with the *Head of the Redeemer*. *Constantine and St Helen* and *Baptism of Christ* by Cima da Conegliano are there, as is a *Last Supper* by Paris Bordone. **Map p. 146, 3C**

San Francesco della Vigna This large 16th-C church, built to a design by Jacopo Sansovino, has a noble classical façade by Andrea Palladio based on a complex arrangement of superimposed temple fronts. The vast Latin cross interior contains numerous masterpieces. Over the first altar of the south transept is the one work that can be attributed with certainty to Fra' Antonio da Negroponte, a *Madonna Adoring the Child* painted in the 1450s in a curious retro style; in the sanctuary are monuments to Doge Andrea Gritti and his circle, possibly by Sansovino; in the chapel on the north of the sanctuary, outstanding sculptures by Pietro Lombardo and pupils (1495–1510); in the Cappella Santa, entered from the north transept, *Madonna and Child with Saints* by Giovanni Bellini (signed and dated 1507); and in the fifth north chapel another *Madonna and Saints*, the Giustinian Altarpiece by Paolo Veronese, and the earliest of his masterpieces to be seen in Venice (1551). **Map p. 146, 3A**

Arsenale The Arsenale was once the greatest shipyard in the world. From 1155 it gave birth to the Venetian galleys, the basis of the Republic's economic and political power. From here, also, comes the modern European word *'arsenal'*—a corruption of the Arabic *darsina'a*, meaning workshop. Dante described this once-bustling dockyard in the *Inferno* (xxi), comparing the boiling pitch used for caulking hulls to the pitch that awaited corrupt barterers of public offices. The Museo Correr (see p. 24) is a good place to go if you want to know more about the Arsenale and its activities.

The complex is usually closed to the public, except when the *corderie*— huge buildings originally designed for the storage of rigging—are used for an exhibition. Part of the complex can be seen, however, from Vaporetto 52, which runs along the canal inside. The land entrance is marked by a doorway of 1460, considered the first work of the Venetian Renaissance, surmounted by a large lion of St Mark. **Map 146, 3A**

IN THE LAGOON

Giudecca Delightfully off the beaten track, the Giudecca is a long, narrow island originally known as Spinalonga ('Long Spine'). Its present name possibly derives from the Jewish community that lived here in the 13th C, although there is much debate about this. By the 16th C it had become a place of lush gardens, aristocratic homes and quiet convents. Following the decline of the Venetian aristocracy and the suppression of the convents, the far end of the island was gradually given over to house barracks, prisons and factories. Today its simple houses are home to many of Venice's boatmen. The quay along the inner, southern side of the island takes different names as it goes along, but always offers splendid views across the channel to San Marco and the Riva degli Schiavoni. The entire section from the Rio di San Biagio canal, on the island's western tip, to the Zitelle church, on the east, is almost tourist-free, and gives a sense of a simpler, original Venice. **Map p. 149, 3A–C**

eat

IN CASTELLO

€ **Al Portego** Castello 6015, San Lio. 041 522 9038. This small, wood-panelled osteria offers a good selection of wine and cichetti as well as simple pasta dishes and *risotti*. It's a cheerful, comfortable place, so don't mind if it's crowded—push your way in and up to the bar for a great snacking experience. Closed Sun, 25 Dec and in June. **Map 124, 3C**

Antica Trattoria Bandierette Castello 6671, Barbaria de la Tole. 041 522 0619. Close to Santi Giovani e Paolo is this unassuming trattoria, frequented by the Venetians for its good, reasonably priced seafood. The atmosphere is plain and simple, with no attempts at elegance, but it's a place to have good food without frills. Closed Sun and late Dec–early Jan. **Map p. 146, 2A**

Dai Tosi Castello 738, Secco Marina. 041 523 7102. This great pizzeria is popular with local families. Its out-of-the-way location in a working class neighbourhood means it's not crammed with tourists, and the price of the pizzas means it's good for any budget. Lots of people go here during the Biennale, but it's worth a visit any time of year. Closed Mon and in July-Aug. **Map p. 148, 2B**

€€ **Al Covo** Castello 3968, Campiello della Pescaria. 041 522 3812. A serious place for serious gourmets, Al Covo is an excellent place

for seafood tucked into a quiet lane behind the Riva degli Schiavoni. Dishes are exquisitely prepared using only the freshest ingredients and a large dose of creativity—and save room for dessert. Closed Wed and Thur, late Dec–early Jan, and Aug. **Map p 146, 3C**

Al Mascaron Castello 5525, Calle Lunga Santa Maria Formosa. 041 522 5995. Everybody knows Mascaron as an informal dinner place with paper placemats and a casual atmosphere. It serves the best of traditional Venetian cuisine, and don't be dismayed by the confusing menu. Once a wine bar, demand for the hot dishes was such that it's now a well established restaurant. Closed Sun and winter. **Map p. 146, 1B**

Alle Testiere Castello 5801, Calle del Mondo Nuovo. 041 522 7220. This place is tiny, with only four tables, but the food is excellent. An intimate (of course) and friendly place, you don't need to worry about menus here—the chef and waiters are mainly interested in absolute freshness and quality and there's always something different on offer. Closed Aug and winter. **Map p. 34, 2B**

ON GUIDECCA

€€ **Harry's Dolci** Giudecca 773, Fondamenta San Biaga. 041 522 4844. Harry's Dolci has the same impeccable level of cuisine and service as Harry's Bar, but is less formal, with tables on the water in summer. In spite of the name, it's a full restaurant, and has a lovely view across the canal to Dorsoduro. Sip a cocktail as *vaporetti* chug by. Closed Tue. **Opposite the Zattere on Giudecca's north bank**

Mistrà Giudecca 212A, Fondamenta San Giacomo. 041 522 0743. Mistrà is gourmet's delight in a former warehouse on the unvisited south side of the Giudecca. It specialises in Ligurian cuisine, that refined style from the sandy beaches and high hills around Genoa. As usual, fish is central here, although the game dishes are also excellent. Closed Mon, Tue, and in Jan-Feb. **Map p. 149, 3C**

WINE BARS

€ **Alla Mascareta** Castello 5183, Calle Lunga Santa Maria Formosa. Now that Al Mascaron is a restaurant, those in search of a wine bar have to walk down the street to Alla Mascareta. This relaxed place is for serious wine aficionados, and serves the best vintages from Friuli and the Veneto. **Map 34, 3A**

CAFÉS

€ **Chiusso** Castello 3306, Salizzada dei Greci. A tiny place serving the freshest pastries and delicious cappuccino. It's part of the Antichi Pasticceri Venexiani chain. **Map p. 146, 2B**

Da Bonifacio Castello 4237, Calle degli Albanesi. Hidden away in a narrow lane behind the Hotel Danieli, this pasticceria is much loved by the Venetians for its traditional pastries and, more importantly, its aperitifs. If you don't think drinking in a bakery seems usual, just watch the people around you and you'll soon see just how appropriate it is. **Map 34, 3B**

Rosa Salva Castello 6779, Campo Santi Giovanni e Paolo. Venice's best pastries, ice cream and hot chocolate are to be had at this venerable establishment, in historic old rooms on a beautiful square. This family-run shop also offers catering services with good, old-fashioned verve and dedication. **Map p. 34, 1A**

shop

BOOKS

Filippi Castello 5284, 5763, Calle Casselleria. This venerable Venetian publisher offers new, used and antique editions of its own and others' books—many dealing with Venetian art and architecture, music, dance and theatre. One of the best things they offer is a facsimile of Francesco Sansovino's 1581 *Venezia*. Sansovino, son of architect Jacopo, is credited with writing the first 'travel guide' to Venice, for which we have to thank him. **Map 34, 2B**

CRAFTS

Anticlea Castello 4719A, Calle San Provolo. This shop has an intriguing selection of antiques and the Venetian glass beads known as *perle veneziane*. The tiny round glass beads known as *conterie*, the cylindrical seeds known as *pivette* and the long, silver-lined *mezza linea* are prized by beaders the world over. The fact that they are made of glass means wonderful, rich colours and idiosyncrasies of shape and size, an inspiration and a challenge for crafting. **Map p. 136, 1B**

Laboratorio Artigiano Maschere Castello 6656, Barbaria delle Tole. Of course, as everyone now knows, the Carnivale of Venice is a reimagined tradition, but that doesn't mean that the crafts inspired by the season are any less stunning. Giorgio Clanetti's Laboratorio Artigiano Maschere is one place to stop for beautifully crafted papier-mâché and leather masks and objets d'art. **Map p. 146, 2A**

FOOD & WINE

Colonna Castello 5595, Calle della Fava. This *bottiglieria*, or wine shop, one of Venice's most established, has a wide selection of regional and Italian wines. It also ships all over the world, so you can pick out some bottles and just unpack them when you arrive home. The friendly staff are quite helpful in giving you tips on which of the Veneto wines you'll like, whether it's a hearty red, a dry white or a delicate Prosecco. **Map p. 34, 2A**

Nave de Oro 1 Castello 5786, Calle Mondo Nuovo. Nave de Oro is a group of wine shops that offers a wide selection of wines and distilled liquors. Stop by No. 1 with an empty bottle and fill up with one of a number of local reds or whites. The price is by the litre and it's the cheapest way to get Veneto grape. **Map p. 34, 2B**

Vino e...Vini Castello 3301, Calle dei Furlani. This is an elegant, pleasant shop with a great selection of Italian and foreign wines, both by the litre and (perhaps more convenient when you're travelling) by the bottle. **Map p. 146, 3B**

THE HOME

Il Milione Castello 6025, Campo Santa Marina. 041 241 0722. Marco Polo was known by the epithet 'Il Milione', or 'the million'. The epithet came from the book he wrote of his travels, which was thought so outrageous that it was a million lies. This shop, selling handcrafted lamps in the Beaux Arts tradition, is just off the street named for the explorer. Here Daniele Zampedri recreates the style of Fortuny using delicate materials. **Map p. 34, 2A**

MUSIC

Regazzo Strumenti Musicali Castello 4700A, Campo San Provolo. Regazzo is a dealer of musical instruments large and small, but with a particular focus on the piano—a souvenir, unfortunately, a little too big for most suitcases. Still, it's a treat to come here and see the beautiful lines of top quality instruments made with dedicated artistry. **Map p. 146, 1A**

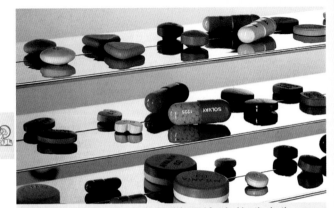

Damien Hirst *Standing Alone on the Precipice and Overlooking the Arctic Wastelands of Pure Terror* (1999-2000) **detail**

La Biennale

The La Biennale di Venezia is perhaps the most famous art event in the world, with celebrated exhibitions in visual arts, cinema, theatre, music and architecture. These events, which draw immense international crowds, usually take place between June and September in odd years.

It has a long and distinguished history. In 1893, the city council passed a resolution on the creation of a biennial exhibition of Italian art. The decision was soon made to invite foreign artists and two years later work was begun on the Palazzo dell'Esposizione (**Map p. 148, 2-3C**). Belgium was the first to open a national pavilion, in 1909, and other countries soon followed. In 1930, the Biennale became a state-run event and received more funding, expanding to include music, cinema and theatre as well as its main event, the International Art Exhibition and its associated awards. Exhibitors in 2003 included top artists such as Damien Hirst (see picture), Gilbert and George, Gustav Metzger and others.

The festival website at www.labiennale.org has information about the programs and events, or call 041 521 8711.

entertainment

INFORMATION
TICKETS
VENUES
TOURS
FESTIVALS
THEATRES
NIGHTLIFE

WHERE TO GET INFORMATION

Un Ospite di Venezia ('A Guest in Venice') is a free, bilingual monthly publication listing everything you need to know to get around. It includes information on exhibitions, performances, sporting events, trade fairs and street markets, as well as useful guides to restaurants, shopping and fun things to do in Venice. It's available at hotels and APT offices and there is an online version at www.unospitedivenezia.it.

WHERE TO GET TICKETS

Box Office (www.boxoffice.it) provides advance booking and ticket sales for many events. Their sales points in Venice are: **Dicottomq** Dorsoduro 3804. 041 275 0170, www.dicottomq.it; **Agenzia Viaggi Kele & Teo** San Marco 4930. 041 520 88722; **Park View Viaggi** Santa Croce 210A. 041 715144, www.parkviaggivenezia.it

VENUES

CLASSICAL MUSIC

Basilica della Salute Dorsoduro, Campo della Salute; vaporetto 1 to Salute. Concerts of religious music, primarily organ

Church of San Giacometto San Polo, Mercati di Rialto; vaporetto 1 or 82 to Rialto. 041 426 6559. The Antonio Vivaldi Ensemble plays Vivaldi, Mozart, Handel and Albinoni in one of the oldest churches in Venice.

Church of San Vidal Campo San Vidal; vaporetto 1 or 82 to Accademia. 041 277 0561, www.interpretiveneziani.com. Orchestra Interpreti Veneziani's chamber music season, with music by Vivaldi, Paganini, Lorenzetti, Bach, Mozart and others

Palazzo Albrizzi Cannaregio 4118; vaporetto 1 to Ca' d'Oro. 041 523 2544, www.acitve.com. Piano recitals

Palazzo delle Prigioni Castello, Ponte Paglia; vaporetto 1, 51 or 52 to San Zaccaria. 041 984 252, www.collegiumducale.com. The Collegium Ducale concert series, well-known Baroque music

Scuola Grande dei Carmini Near Campo Santa Margherita; vaporetto 1 to Ca' Rezzonico. Ensemble Antonio Vivaldi, in period costumes.

Scuola Grande di San Teodoro Campo San Salvador; vaporetto 1 or 82 to Rialto, 041 521 0294, www.imusiciveneziani.com. Vivaldi in period costume; also Albinoni, Mozart, Donizetti, Pergolesi, Galuppi, Verdi.

Teatro Malibran Campiello Malibran. 041 241 8033, 041 2424, www.teatrolafenice.it. Società Veneziana dei Concerti's orchestra and chamber music season

Teatro La Fenice San Marco 1965. 041.241 8033, www.teatrolafenice.it. The restored La Fenice (see p. 36) has an opera and symphony concert season. Some events are still held at the Palfenice tent theatre on the Tronchetto.

CONTEMPORARY

Teatro Fondamenta Nuove Cannaregio 5013 (Fondamente Nuove, Gesuiti; vaporetto 51, 61, 62, or LN). 041 522 44 98, www.teatrofondamenta nuove.it. Risonanze concerts of new contemporary music

WALKING TOURS

Associazione Sant'Apollonia 041 270 2464. Guided tours of churches and monuments not part of the usual itineraries, such as the Basilica of Santa Maria Assunta (Torcello), the churches of San Pantalon, the Carmini, San Trovaso, San Giovanni in Bragora, San Salvador and San Barnaba. Proceeds go to the Venetian Patriarchate.

Chorus – Associazione delle Chiese di Venezia San Polo 2986. 041 275 0462, www.chorusvenezia.org. This association of fifteen of Venice's most important churches offers a guided tour. Proceeds go towards preservation work.

The Hidden Venice of Sherlock Holmes Campo San Stae, Trattoria Antica Sacrestia. 041 523 0749, 349 158 3278 (ask for Ivo Lombardo). Tour of the places in *Sherlock Holmes in Venice*. Sun 11 am, booking required.

Venus in Venice, Places of Love 041 630761, 333 854 7763. New series of guided tours by poet Lucio Marco Zorzi, highlighting historical curiosities and interwoven with poetry recitals.

CELEBRATIONS

CARNIVAL

Carnevale draws merry-makers who come for the chance to parade through the streets in fancy dress and masks. A special event since the 11th C, its popularity (and excesses) peaked in the 18th C, then declined until relatively recently. The 1980s saw the reinvention of the carnival as a major tourist attraction. Today this animated, exciting celebration, whose masks and costumes endow participants with the freedom of anonymity, draws revellers from all over the world. Locals, alas, tend to hide from the mobs during the 10-day Lenten onslaught. Dates for upcoming carnivals: *2005* 1 Feb–8 Feb; *2006* 21 Feb–28 Feb; *2007* 13 Feb–20 Feb

Festa del Redentore Third Sun of July, www.comune.venezia.it/turismo. Venice commemorates the end of the plague of 1576 with an impressive bridge of boats across the Canale della Giudecca, over which people walk to the church of Redentore to attend Mass and then to the lagoon to watch fireworks.

Festa della Madonna della Salute Basilica della Salute, 21 Nov. 041 522 5558. Traditional 'pilgrimage' to fulfil a vow taken during a plague in the 17th C, to the famous church built by Longhena.

Festa di San Marco - Il Bòcolo 25 April, www.comune.venezia.it/turismo. Mark is the patron saint of Venice and his feast day celebration includes a gondola race in the Bacino di San Marco from Sant'Elena to Punta della Dogana, High Mass and additional events.

La Sensa Sunday after Ascension Day. It culminates in a ceremony recalling the traditional marriage between the Doge and the sea, celebrated by a parade of gondolas.

STREET FAIRS

Antique Art Street Fair Campo San Maurizio. 041 988810. June, Sept and Dec. Traditional antique art market, offering objects and collections in Liberty and other 20th-C styles.

SPORT

National Championship B-League Football Stadio P.L. Penzo, Isola di Sant'Elena (vaporetto 1 or 52). 041 238 0711, www.veneziacalcio.it. For those who just can't do without.

Su and zo per i Ponti 041 590 4717, www.suezoperiponti.org. A festive 12-km non-competitive run held the second Sun in March. It starts at the Paglia Bridge at 10 am and winds through alleys, across squares and over bridges. Registration €4.

Venice Marathon Stra (Riviera del Brenta) to Venice (S. Marco). Venice-Marathon Club, 041 940644, www.venicemarathon.it. One of the major Italian marathons, held in October.

Regata Storica First Sun in Sept, 041 274 7744, www.comune.venezia.it/turismo. Gondoliers and other boatmen compete in a regatta that starts with an historical procession along the Grand Canal. The most spectacular rowing event of the year.

Burano Regata Burano, Sept. 041 274 7737. One of the more exciting races of the Venetian rowing season, viewed locally as the return match to the Regata Storica.

Vogalonga Two Sundays after Ascension, www.vogalonga.it. Hundreds of boats take part in this 32-km regatta from San Marco to Burano and back.

THEATRE & CINEMA

If you're tired of history, or your feet hurt from tramping a calle, you can catch a film at **Giorgioni Cinema d'Essai**, at Cannaregio 4612 (take vaporetto 1 to Ca' d'Oro), 041 522 6298, which shows first runs in original languages. If you're at the Lido, see first runs and art films at **Astra Multiplex**, Via Corfù 12, 041 522 6298.

If you speak Italian and are in the mood for a play, there are good things to see, including open air performances in the summer. Check **Un Ospite di Venezia** for details (or www.unospitedivenezia.com).

VENICE BY NIGHT

Venice is famously not a city with much of a nightlife. There is, of course, the **Venice Casino** (Cannaregio 2040, Ca' Vendramin Calergi, San Marcuola), which is open during the summer. There are also a few bars with music that stay open late (or at least later), such as **Bacaro Jazz Venezia** (San Marco 5546, Poste Centrali). **Piccolo Mondo** (Dorsoduro 1056A, Accademia) is a disco.

planning

WHEN TO GO
HOW TO GET AROUND
PRACTICALITIES
FOOD AND DRINK
PLACES TO STAY

WHEN TO GO

The best time to visit Venice is late spring (May–June) or early autumn (Sept–Oct). The earlier spring and later autumn months are often wet and unexpectedly chilly, with strong northerly winds. The height of the summer is unpleasantly hot, and winter days are cold and wet.

PASSPORTS AND FORMALITIES

Passports or ID cards are necessary for EU travellers entering Italy. North American travellers must carry passports, but for visits of up to 90 days no visa is required for EU, US or Canadian citizens. Citizens of other countries should check current visa requirements with the nearest Italian consulate before departure.

Italian law requires travellers to carry some form of identification at all times. A stolen or lost passport can be replaced with little trouble by the relevant embassy in Rome. All foreign visitors to Italy must register with the police within three days of arrival; if you are staying at a hotel, this formality is attended to by the management, but if staying with friends or in a private home, you must register in person at the nearest police station (*questura*).

GETTING THERE
BY AIR

Venice's **Marco Polo International Airport** is located on the mainland, 13 km north of the city. Marco Polo handles domestic flights and most international European flights.

General information 041 2609240-2609250

Flight information 041 2609260

Treviso Airport is around 30 km from Venice and handles some European flights. Together the two airports form Italy's third largest (with 6 million passengers annually) and fastest growing airport system.

AIRLINE OFFICE NUMBERS TO CALL FROM VENICE

Air Dolomiti 800 013366
Air France 848 884466
Air Lingus 02 76000080
Air One 848 848880
Alitalia 848 865641-2-3
Alpi Eagles 041 5997788
American Airlines 02 69682464
Austrian Airlines 02 80663095
British Airways 199 712266
Delta Air Lines 800 477999
Iberia 848 826236
KLM 02 218981
Lufthansa 02 80663025
Maersk 0045 70107474
SAS 02 72000193
Swisswings 00800 83483400
Volare 800 454000

BUDGET AIRLINES

Venice is a favourite destination for budget airlines. Some of those that fly there are:

British Midland www.iflybritishmidland.com
Easyjet www.go-fly.com
Ryanair www.ryanair.com
SkyEurope www.skyeurope.com

WEB FARES

There are many agencies offering travel on the web. The best include:

Mobissimo www.mobissimo.com
Expedia www.expedia.co.uk, www.expedia.com
Travelocity www.travelocity.com

BY TRAIN

Information about the **Italian Railways (Trenitalia)** can be obtained in the UK from European Rail Travel Ltd, 020 7387 0444, www.raileurope.co.uk. For direct information and tickets check www.trenitalia.it. Trenitalia Help Desk: +39 06 8833 9537, helpdesk@sipax.com.

In North America, Trenitalia information and tickets can be obtained from European Rail Travel, (877) 257 2887 in the US and (800) 361 RAIL in Canada, or www.raileurope.com.

BY CAR

You can reach Venice from the west, the direction of Padua, by the A4 or 11; from the north, the direction of Treviso, by the A27 and Highway 13 (the latter is faster from central Treviso); and the east, the direction of Trieste, by the A4 or Highway 14. All roads from the mainland terminate at Piazzale Roma.

CAR PARKS

Motorists have to leave their vehicles in a garage or an open car park (charges vary according to the size of the vehicle, but the rates are per day and space is very limited, especially in summer). The most convenient garages are at Piazzale Roma, but there are also garages and huge open car parks at Isola del Tronchetto. Frequent vaporetto services serve all of these. In summer, and at Easter and Carnival, parking is usually available also at San Giuliano and Fusina.

GETTING TO THE CITY CENTRE

Airport buses link the airport terminals and the car park at Piazzale Roma, and there are regular boat connections between Venice Marco Polo airport, San Marco (Giardinetti landing stage) and the Lido. If you are carrying a lot of baggage, you might want to consider a water taxi, an expensive option but one that will take you directly to the landing nearest your hotel.

ACTV buses run **from Marco Polo airport** to the train station at Mestre-Venezia (ATVO Fly Bus, roughly every fifteen minutes, and ACTV line 15, at roughly half-hour intervals) and to Piazzale Roma (ACTV Line 5, leaving roughly every half hour). Tickets may be purchased at the airport at a booth in the arrivals hall, 8 am–12 am, or on the bus. Information: 041 541 5180.

ATVO buses run **from Treviso Giannino Ancilotto Airport**. Tickets may be purchased at the airport at a booth in the arrivals hall, 8 am–12 am, or on the bus. Information: 041 520 5530, www.atvo.it.

Alilaguna provides a boat shuttle from Marco Polo Airport to various stops in Venice, Murano and the Lido. Tickets cost €5–10, depending on the stop, and may be purchased at the airport at a booth in the arrivals hall, 8 am–12 am. Information: 041 541 5180, www.alilaguna.it

Water taxis are operated by the Consorzio Motoscafi Venezia. This is the nicest and the easiest way to get to Venice, but also the priciest. Information: 041 541 5084, 041 522 2303, www.motoscafivenezia.it

Ground taxis are available from Marco Polo Airport to the car park at Piazzale Roma. Information: Radiotaxi 041 936222

GETTING AROUND

There are only two ways to get around Venice—by land and by water—and neither of them is very fast. If you can manage to go from your starting point to your destination without making a wrong turn, walking is probably the most practical means of locomotion. The trouble is, Venice's maze-like street plan prevents out-of-towners like you and me from getting from here to there on the first try. (If you wish to walk through Venice without carrying luggage, shopping bags, or other encumbrances, you can hire a *portabagagli* (porter), to do the work for you. Your hotel will have details.)

THE STREETS OF VENICE

Calle, *salizzada*, *fondamenta*—the streets of Venice have as many names as they do shapes and sizes, but confusing as they seem, there's reason behind the names. The oldest main streets of the islands, ones originally planned as paved, major thoroughfares, are known as *salizzade*. These were used before the urban build-up of the marshy islets. As dry land became a premium, streets were created on the edges of the canals by extending them on wooden pillars driven into the mud, creating a *fondamenta*. Where the demand for space became even more urgent, canals were actually filled in, and a street resulting from this process is known as a *rio terrà*, or 'land canal'. The tiny streets that developed in the spaces around the buildings of the city are mostly known as *calle*, from the Latin for 'path'. The *campi*, or squares, were once fields in the inner parts of the 117 islets that made up the bulk of Venice. There was often a church at one edge, and as the city developed, shops serving the parish began to cluster there.

BY PUBLIC TRANSPORT
BY VAPORETTO

The vaporetto (water bus) is the most convenient way of getting around town, but it is painfully slow and in the high season (May–Oct) jam-packed with passengers.

Timetables, tickets and fares Timetables are posted at most landing stages and published monthly in the tourist board's helpful booklet, Un *Ospite di Venezia* (see Information offices, below). Tickets can be bought during working hours at most landing stages and from shops displaying the logo of the municipal transport company ACTV, or on board after hours. There are discounts for round-trip, 24-hour and 3-day tickets. Information: 041 272 2111, www.actv.it

The **Venice Card** (see p. 183) also covers transportation on the vaporetti for a set period of days.

BY MOTOSCAFO

Motoscafi (water taxis) are the fastest and most exclusive vehicles in Venice. Point-to-point service in town is metred, and there are fixed rates (published in **Un Ospite di Venezia**) for the most common destinations outside the city centre. There are taxi stands on the quays in front of the train station, Piazzale Roma, Rialto, San Marco and other places, or you can call for one.

Radio Taxi 041 522 2303, 041 713112
Coop Veneziana 041 716124
Coop Serenissima 041 522 1265, 041 522 8538

Società Narduzzi Solemar 041 520 0838
Società Marco Polo 041 966170
Società Sotoriva 041 520 9586
Società Serenessima 041 522 4281
Venezia Taxi 041 723009
At San Marco (Molo) 041 522 9750

BY GONDOLA

Gondole can be hired for a leisurely tour of the city, at standard rates or on a custom service basis. In the latter case, be sure to agree upon the duration and price of your ride before setting out. There are gondola stands at the station, Piazzale Roma, Calle Vallaresso (San Marco), Riva degli Schiavoni and other places around town.

BY TRAGHETTO

Traghetti (gondola ferries) offer a handy way of getting across the Grand Canal without walking all the way to one of the bridges (there are only three: at the train station, Rialto and the Accademia). You'll see yellow signs marked *traghetto* here and there as you wander the city. They are extremely cheap and quite a lot of fun, for in all but the roughest weather you ride standing up. Most operate from early morning until late afternoon. Furthermore, some vaporetti operate as traghetti on short, single-stop trips. Cases in which a traghetto fare applies will appear on the tariff list at the ticket booth.

MONEY

In Italy, the monetary unit is the euro (€). There are banks with ATMs accepting Visa and MasterCard, Maestro and Cirrus cards throughout the city, and most credit cards are now generally accepted in hotels, shops and restaurants.

Cash can be changed at banks, post offices, travel agencies and some hotels, restaurants and shops, though the rate of exchange can vary considerably from place to place. Banks are open Mon–Fri, 8.30 am–1.30 pm and 2.30 pm–4 pm. Afternoon opening hours may vary from bank to bank, and many banks close early (about 11 am) on days preceding national holidays.

Exchange offices are usually open seven days a week at airports and most main railway stations. A limited amount of euros can be obtained from conductors on international trains and at certain stations. For small amounts of money, the difference between hotel and bank rates may be negligible, as banks tend to take a fixed commission on transactions.

WEB RESOURCES
CITY SITES
The official website of the Venice tourist office (Azienda di Promozione Turistica di Venezia) is **www.turismovenezia.it** and the municipal site of the Comune di Venezia is **www.comune.venezia.it.**

GENERAL TOURIST SITES
Regione del Veneto, Assessorato al Turismo: **turismo.regione.veneto.it**
Primitaly: **www.primitaly.it/veneto**
Meeting Venice: **www.meetingvenice.it**
Alata: **www.alata.it**

TRANSPORT
ACTV public transportation, including vaporetto lines: **www.actv.it**
Alilaguna shuttles to the airport: **www.alilaguna.it.**

FUN
Venice Word, general and entertainment information:
www.veniceword.com

La Biennale di Venezia: **www.labiennale.org**

All about gondolas at Gondola Venezia: **www.gondolavenezia.it**

INFORMATION OFFICES AND PUBLICATIONS
The **Azienda di Promozione Turistica di Venezia (APT)** provides information about hotel accommodation, money changing, railway and motorway connections, airline companies and consulate addresses. They also provide the opening time of places to visit and a schedule of exhibitions, theatres and concerts. A mail, phone and fax information service is also provided to Italian and foreign users.

Offices: San Marco 71, Calle Ascensione, 041 529 8740; Stazione Santa Lucia, 041 529 8727; Aeroporto Marco Polo, 041 260 6111

Un Ospite di Venezia ('A Guest in Venice') is a free, bilingual monthly publication available at hotels and APT offices. It has good listings of the month's exhibitions, performances, sporting events, trade fairs and street markets, and a regular section covering restaurants, shopping and things to do in Venice. There is an online version at www.unospitedivenezia.it.

MUSEUM AND DISCOUNT CARDS

There are various cards that give you discounts in Venice. It's a little confusing to figure out which you want, but it's well worth getting one that fits the trip you plan.

The **Museum Card** gives free entrance to the Museums of San Marco, which belong to the Musei Civici Veneziani group. This includes the Palazzo Ducale, the Museo Correr, the Museo Archeologico Nazionale and the Biblioteca Marciana. You can get the Museum card at participating museums for €11.

There are two types of **Venice Card**, Orange and Blue. Each has two different age categories and three categories for lengths of stay, so finding which one works for you can be complicated. Still, it can be worth it, as the discounts are significant. It is available online at www.venicecard.it or at Venice Card offices at the Piazzale Roma car park, Santa Lucia Station, Marco Polo Airport and Punta Sabbioni port.

Venice Card Blue
Free transport on the vaporetti
Discounts at participating shops and restaurants
Free use of the public toilets

Venice Card Orange
Free transport on the vaporetti
Free admission to the Musei Civici:

Palazzo Ducale	Museo Correr
Torre dell'Orologio	Ca' Rezzonico
Palazzo Mocenigo	Casa di Carlo Goldoni
Ca' Pesaro	Museo Fortuny
Museo del Vetro	Museo del Merletto
Museo di Storia Naturale	

Free admission to the Museo Archeologico
Discounts at participating shops and restaurants
Free use of the public toilets

You can buy the Venice Cards, Blue or Orange, for either 1, 3 or 7 days. The 'Junior' price is for those under thirty, the 'Senior' price for those thirty and older.

Days	€Jr	€Sr	€Jr	€Sr
1	9	14	18	28
3	22	29	35	47
7	49	51	61	68

The **Rolling Venice Card** gives all benefits of the Blue Venice Card, plus discounts at hostels and campgrounds, and is only for people under 29.

The **Chorus Pass** gives entry to 15 churches belonging to the Associazione Chiese di Venezia. The pass is €8 (€5 if you have any variety of Venice Card) and can be purchased at any of the participating churches. www.chorusvenezia.org

S. Alvise	Madonna dell'Orto
S. Stae	S. Giovanni Elemosinario
S. Maria dei Miracoli	S. Maria Formosa
S. Pietro di Castello	S. Maria del Giglio
S. Stefano	SS. Redentore
Gesuati	S. Sebastiano
S. Polo	S. Giacomo dell'Orio

SALES TAX REBATES

If you're a non-EU resident, you can claim sales tax rebates on purchases made in Italy, provided the total expenditure is more than €150. Ask the vendor for a receipt describing the goods acquired and get it checked and stamped by Italian customs on leaving Italy (take extra time for this). Then send the receipt back to the vendor when you get home, within 90 days of purchase. The vendor will forward the sales tax rebate (currently 20% on most goods) to your home address.

TELEPHONE AND POSTAL SERVICES

Stamps are sold at tobacconists (tabacchi) and post offices. Correspondence can be sent post restante by adding 'Fermo Posta' to the name of the locality.

Card-operated public phones are becoming increasingly common in Italy. Cards offering €2.50 or €5 in prepaid calls (particularly convenient for phoning abroad) are available at post offices, tobacconists and some news-stands. For all calls in Italy, local and long-distance, dial the area code (for instance, 080 for Bari), then the telephone number. For international and intercontinental calls, dial 00 plus the country code, then the area code.

Venice area code 041
Dialling the UK from Italy (0044) + number without the initial zero
Dialling the US from Italy (001) + number
Dialling Venice from the UK (0039) + number
Dialling Venice from the US (011 39) + number

You can reach an AT&T operator at 800-172-444, MCI at 800-90-5825, or Sprint at 800-172-405. For directory assistance call 12 (for numbers in

Italy) or 176 (for international numbers). You can receive a wake-up call on your phone by dialling 114 and following the prompts (in Italian).

HEALTH AND INSURANCE

British citizens, as members of the EU, can claim health treatment in Italy if they have an E111 form (issued by the DSS). There are also a number of private holiday health insurance policies. Italy has no medical programme covering US or Canadian citizens, who are advised to take out an insurance policy before travelling.

EMERGENCIES AND PERSONAL SECURITY

Police 113 (Polizia di Stato) or 112 (Carabinieri)

Fire brigade 115

Medical emergencies 118

Lost and found Marco Polo Airport 041 260 6436; Santa Lucia Station 848 888088

Lost or stolen credit cards American Express 055 238 2876; Mastercard 800 872 050; Visa 800 877 232

Road assistance 116

EMBASSIES AND CONSULATES

Canada Riviera Ruzzante 25, Padua. 049 878 1147. Mon–Thur 8.30 am–12.30 pm and 1.15 pm–5.30 pm; Fri 8.30 am–1 pm.

Netherlands (Honarary) San Marco 2888. 041 528 3416

United Kingdom (Honarary) Dorsoduro 1051. 041 522 7207

United States Via Prinipe Amedeo 2/10, Milan. 02 29035. Mon–Fri 9 am–12.30 pm and 1.30 pm–2.30 or 3.30 pm

EMERGENCY ROOMS

Ospedale Civile di Venezia Cannaregio, Campo Santi Giovanni e Paolo, 041 529 4111

Ospedale al Mare Lido di Venezia Lungomare d'Annunzio 1. 041 529 4111

Ospedale Civile di Mestre Via Ospedale, Venezia Mestre. 041 260 7111

DOCTORS

Guardia Medica 24 hour Medical Service. 041 5344411

LATE-NIGHT PHARMACIES

These pharmacies take turns staying open, so phone before going.

San Marco

Alla Madonna San Marco 5310, Campo San Bartolomeo. 041 522 4196

Alla Vecchia e al Cedro Imperiale San Marco 4598, San Luca. 041 522 2638

Internazionale San Marco 2067, Calle Larga XXII Marzo. 041 522 2311

Dorsoduro

Santa Margherita Dorsoduro 3692, Campo Santa Margherita. 041 522 3872

Santa Croce

San Francesco Santa Croce 181, Fondamenta Tolentini. 041 528 6936

San Polo

Ai Due San Marchi San Polo 2498, Campo San Stin. 041 522 5865

Cannaregio

All'Anconetta Cannaregio 1825, Campo Anconetta. 041 720 622

Alle Due Colonne Cannaregio 6045, Campo San Canciano, 041 522 5411

Al Re d'Italia Cannaregio 3823a, San Felice. 041 522 5970

Antica Santa Fosca Cannaregio 2233A. 041 720 600

Castello

Al Basilisco Castello 1778, Via Garibaldi. 041 522 4109

Croce di Malta Castello 3470, Ponte Sant'Antonin. 041 522 2653

CRIME

Pickpocketing is a widespread problem in towns all over Italy, and it is always advisable not to carry valuables in your pocket and to be particularly careful on public transport. Never wear conspicuous jewellery, including necklaces and expensive watches. Crime should be reported at once to the police, or the local Carabinieri office. A detailed statement has to be given in order to get an official document confirming loss or damage (essential for insurance claims). Interpreters are provided.

DISABLED TRAVELLERS

All new public buildings are obliged by law to provide easy access and specially designed facilities for the disabled. Unfortunately, the conversion of historical buildings, including many museums and monuments, is made problematic by structural impediments such as narrow pavements. Barriers therefore continue to exist in many cases. Hotels that are equipped to accommodate the disabled are indicated in an annual list of hotels published by the tourist board. Airports and railway stations provide assistance and certain trains are equipped to transport wheelchairs. Cars with disabled drivers or passengers are allowed access to the centre of town (normally closed to traffic), where special parking places are reserved for them. For further information, contact an APT office (see p. 183).

FOOD AND DRINK
THE CUISINE OF THE VENETO

Venice is a city of the sea, and in no way is that more obvious than in its cuisine. You'll eat a lot of fish in Venice, and it will almost always be fresh and high quality. Local specialities include *granseola* (lagoon crabs), *sarde in saor* (marinated sardines) and *seppioline nere* (cuttlefish cooked in their own ink). An outstanding seafood dish is the *brodetto di pesce* or *boreto di Grado*—rigorously *bianco* (without tomatoes), which testifies to its origins in an age before the discovery of America.

Rice is served in a variety of ways in Venice, especially with seafood and vegetables. Classic specialities are *risi e bisi* (risotto with peas) and *risotto nero* (coloured and flavoured with the ink of cuttlefish). Thick soups are also popular, the best of which is *pasta e fasioi* (pasta and beans), which is eaten lukewarm. The classical pasta e fasioi once called for *bigoli*, a local variant of spaghetti made with water and buckwheat or wholewheat flour, but nowadays other types of pasta are used, too.

Cornmeal polenta is another staple, often served with the famous *fegato alla venziana* (calves' liver and onions). *Tiramisù*, a combination of creamy mascarpone cheese, finger biscuits, coffee and cocoa, is the favourite dessert, though you'll also find rich cakes and pastries of Austrian inspiration.

Cicchetti are those little bite-sized pieces you'll see in most wine bars, heaped into appetising piles behind the bar. They can range from fried squid to sweet cheese and jam and are an excellent way to do a lot of tasting without stuffing yourself.

Venetian restaurants will also serve you dishes from elsewhere in the region. Distinctive dishes from Padua include rice and tagliatelli in *brodo d'anatra* (duck broth), and *risotto con rovinasassi* (chicken giblets). The best-known speciality of Vicenza is *baccalà alla vicentina* (salt cod stewed with milk and onions and grilled polenta), while Veronese specialities include gnocchi in butter or tomato sauce, or topped with *pastizzada de*

caval (horsemeat stewed with aromatic herbs). Among Veronese sweets, the most delectable is certainly the great fluffy cake *pandoro*. The leading role in Trevisan cuisine is played by the long, narrow heads of Treviso's red lettuce, radicchio trevigiano, which is eaten in salads, grilled, fried or in risotto.

The best wines of the Veneto are labelled DOC, *di origine controllata*. The reds are typically full-bodied and the whites dry, but both go well with rich, hearty Venetian cuisine. The lightly sparkling Prosecco white, which can also be called Prosecco di Valdobbiadene and Prosecco di Conegliano, is a favourite aperitif throughout Italy. Mix it with the juice and pulp of white peaches, and you get a Bellini, the famous cocktail invented at Harry's Bar on Piazza San Marco.

RESTAURANTS, WINE BARS AND CAFÉS

Italian restaurants are usually good and inexpensive. Generally speaking, the least pretentious ristorante (restaurant), trattoria (small restaurant) or osteria (inn or tavern) provides the best value. The restaurants listed in each chapter have been chosen for the quality and distinction of their cuisine and the extent of their wine lists; even the simplest are quite good. Like hotels, they have been rated by price: consider an expensive (€€€) meal one costing €45 or more, a moderate (€€) meal €20-45, and an inexpensive (€) meal under €20. As a rule, the more exclusive eateries are considerably cheaper at midday. You should telephone for details and make a reservation, as all the establishments listed provide good value for money and are likely to be very popular.

Prices on the menu do not include the cover charge (shown separately, usually at the bottom of the page). The service charge (*servizio*) is sometimes automatically added at the end of the bill, and if it is, tipping is not strictly necessary, but is appreciated. Many simpler establishments do not offer a written menu, and although the choice is limited, the standard of cuisine is usually quite acceptable.

Wine bars provide a good alternative to restaurants for a quick lunch or a mid-afternoon snack. They are also a good place to meet friends in the evening. Most offer a daily selection of wines of varying price, plus *cicheti* and light meals.

Cafés are open from early morning to late at night and serve all sorts of excellent refreshments, usually eaten standing up. As a rule, you must pay the cashier first, then present your receipt to the barman in order to get served. If you sit at a table the charge is usually higher and you will be given waiter service, and don't have to pay first. However, some simple bars have a few tables that can be used with no extra charge, and it is always best to ask before ordering whether there is waiter service or not.

Caffè or espresso, can be ordered *lungo* (diluted), *corretto* (with a liqueur) or *macchiato* (with a dash of hot milk). A cappuccino is an espresso with more hot milk than a caffè macchiato and is generally considered a breakfast drink. A glass of hot milk with a dash of coffee in it, called *latte macchiato*, is another early-morning favourite. In summer, many drink *caffè freddo* (iced coffee).

OPENING TIMES
GALLERIES, MUSEUMS AND CHURCHES

The opening times of museums and monuments are given in the text, but they often change without warning. Although the tourist board keeps updated timetables of most museums, you should allow enough time for variations when planning a visit to a museum or monument. National museums and monuments are usually open every day, 8.15 am–6.50 pm, plus evening hours in summer. Churches open quite early in the morning (often for 6 am Mass) but are normally closed for a considerable period during the middle of the day (from around noon to anywhere from 3 pm to 5 pm). Some churches now ask that sightseers do not enter during a service, but normally visitors may do so, provided they are silent and do not approach the altar in use. At all times they are expected to cover their legs and arms, and generally dress with decorum. In Holy Week most of the pictures are covered.

SHOPS

All shops are generally open Mon–Sat, 8.30 am or 9.00 am–1 pm and 3.30 pm or 4 pm–7.30 or 8 pm. Shops selling clothes and other goods are usually closed on Mon morning and food shops on Weds afternoon. This changes from mid-June to mid-Sept, when all shops are closed instead on Sat afternoon.

PUBLIC HOLIDAYS

   1 January
  25 April (Liberation Day)
  Easter Sunday and Easter Monday
   1 May (Labour Day)
  24 June (St John the Baptist)
  15 August (Assumption)
   1 November (All Saints' Day)
   8 December (Immaculate Conception)
  25 December (Christmas Day)
  26 December (St Stephen)

TIME

Italy is one hour ahead of Greenwich Mean Time, six hours ahead of Eastern Standard Time and nine hours ahead of Pacific Standard Time in the US. Daylight saving time in Italy usually runs from April to Oct.

TIPPING

A service charge of 15%–18% is added to hotel bills, but is usually already part of an inclusive price. Still, it is customary to leave an additional tip in any case. Depending on the category of your hotel, a tip of €1–2 is suggested for any hotel staff, except the concierge, who may expect €2–3.

Restaurants add a service charge of approximately 15% to all bills. It is customary, however, to leave a small tip (5%–10%) for good service. In cafés and bars, leave 15% if you sit at a table (unless the bill already includes service) and 10–20 euro cents if standing at a counter or bar to drink.

At the theatre, opera and concerts, tip ushers 50 cents or more, depending on the price of your seat.

WEIGHTS AND MEASURES

Italians use the metric system of weights and measures. The *metro* is the unit of length, the *grammo* of weight, the ara of land and the *litro* of capacity. Greek-derived prefixes (*deca-, etto-, chilo-*) are used with those names to express multiples; Latin prefixes (*deci-, centi-, milli*) to express fractions (a chilometro=1000 metri, while a millimetro=1000th part of a metro). For approximate calculations, the metro may be taken as 39 inches and the chilometro as 0.6 miles; the litro as 1.75 pints; an etto as 3.5 oz; and the chilo as 2.2 lb.

PLACES TO STAY

The hotels listed, regardless of their cost, have been chosen on the basis of their character or location. All have something special about them—beautiful surroundings or a distinctive atmosphere—and even the humblest are adequately comfortable. Generally speaking, you should expect a double room at an expensive (€€€) hotel to cost €200 or more, at a moderate (€€) hotel €100-200, and at an inexpensive (€) hotel under €100. The local tourist offices will help you find accommodation on the spot, but that's taking a big risk if you're travelling in the high season. You should try to book well in advance, especially if you're planning to travel between May and Oct. Hotels will allow you to claim back part or all of your deposit if you cancel the booking at least 72 hours in advance. Hotels equipped to offer hospitality to the disabled are indicated in the tourist boards' hotel lists.

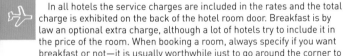

In all hotels the service charges are included in the rates and the total charge is exhibited on the back of the hotel room door. Breakfast is by law an optional extra charge, although a lot of hotels try to include it in the price of the room. When booking a room, always specify if you want breakfast or not—it is usually worthwhile just to go around the corner to the nearest café for breakfast. Hotels are now obliged by law (for tax purposes) to issue an official receipt to customers and you should not leave the premises without this document.

There are no street addresses in Venice. Mail is delivered by neighbourhood and number (for instance, San Marco 1243), but that's not much help if you're wandering the streets in search of a hotel. For this reason, you'll find two addresses, below, for each hotel: first the postal address, then the (approximate) street location, in parentheses.

Most of Venice's luxury hotels are arranged in a neat row along the waterfront on either side of San Marco. Moderately priced hotels can be found throughout the city, but good ones are few and far between. The level of comfort and service in inexpensive hotels can be downright disappointing—as is to be expected in a town, like Venice, subject to excessive demand. If you're looking for an adequate place to stay but are short on cash, bear in mind that several of the city's religious communities open their convents to visitors during high season, offering very good accommodation at remarkably low prices. Details from the APT.

B&B accommodation, usually in private homes or villas, may be booked through a central agency. Contact **Caffelletto**, Via di Marciola 23, 50020 San Vincenzo a Torri (Firenze) Italy, 055 7309145, fax 055 768121, www.caffelletto.it; **BedandBreakfast.com**, www.bedandbreakfast.com; or **Bed & Breakfast in Europe**, www.bedandbreakfastineurope.com/italia/en.htm.

SAN MARCO

€€ Flora San Marco 2283a, Calle dei Bergamaschi. 041 520 5844, fax 041 522 8217, www.hotelflora.it. Nicely situated between the Luna and the Gritti, with a beautiful small garden. **Map p. 8, 3C**

La Fenice et des Artistes San Marco 1936, Campiello de la Fenice. 041 523 2333, fax 041 520 3721, www.fenicehotels.com. It really is frequented by artists (there are some original works by 20th-C masters in the lobby). **Map p. 8, 3B**

Locanda Art Decò San Marco 2966, Calle delle Botteghe. 041 277 0558, fax 041 270 2891, www.locandaartdeco.com. Just six delightful, luminous rooms, with art deco furniture; closed Dec–Jan and Aug. **Map p. 8, 2B**

Locanda Fiorita San Marco 3457a, Campiello Novo. 041 523 4754, fax 041 522 8043, www.locandafiorita.com. It's hard to imagine something more charming than this refined little family-run establishment on a tiny square, with outside breakfast seating in summer. **Map p. 8, 2B**

€€€Europa & Regina San Marco 2159, Calle Larga 22 Marzo. 041 520 0477, fax 041 523 1533, www.starwoodhotels.com. Difficult to find by land, but with a private dock on the Grand Canal, on which it fronts. **Map p. 8, 3C**

Gritti Palace San Marco 2467, Campo Santa Maria del Giglio. 041

794611, fax 041 520 0942, www.starwoodhotels.com. Rich in Venetian atmosphere, with summer dining on the Grand Canal. **Map p. 8, 3C**

Luna Baglioni San Marco 1243, Calle Larga del 'Ascensione. 041 528 9840, fax 041 528 7160, www.baglionihotels.com. Quieter and more secluded than the other grand hotels. **Map p. 9, 1B**

Palazzo Sant'Angelo San Marco 3489. 041 241 1452, fax 041 241 1557, www.palazzosantangelo.com. For honeymooners only: four luxurious suites in a tiny, intimate townhouse overlooking the Grand Canal, between San Marco and the Accademia bridge. **Map p. 8, 3A**

DORSODURO

€€ **Accademia** Dorsoduro 1058, Fondamenta Bollani. 041 523 7846, fax 041 523 9152, www.pensioneaccademia.it. Near the Accademia, with a shady garden. **Map p. 50, 3B**

La Calcina Dorsoduro 780, Zattere. 041 520 6466, fax 041 522 7045, www.lacalcina.com. Where Ruskin stayed: the rooms overlooking the Giudecca are among the city's most charming. **Map X, XX**

€€€**Ca' Pisan** Dorsoduro 979A, Rio Terrà Foscarini. 041 240 1411, fax 041 240 1425, www.capisanihotel.it. In a great location just a few paces from the Accademia bridge, boutique hotel offering 14th-C architecture and art deco furnishings. **Map p. 8, 1C**

SAN POLO AND SANTA CROCE

€€ **Ai Due Fanali** Santa Croce 946, Campo San Simeon Grande. 041 718490, fax 041 718344, www.aiduefanali.com. A former religious school with ceiling frescos by Palma Giovane, now a small, quiet place just a short walk from the station, recently renovated with all modern comforts. **Map p. 88, 2A**

Falier Santa Croce 130, Salizzada San Pantalon. 041 710 882, fax 041 520 6554, www.hotelfalier.com. Simple but quite good, especially the top-floor rooms with private terrace, in a delightful residential neighbourhood far from the crowds. **Map p. 88, 1C**

CANNAREGIO

€ **Casa Martini** Cannaregio 1314. 041 717512, fax 041 275 8329, www.casamartini.it. Pleasant bed & breakfast offering old-time Venetian style in air-conditioned modern comfort; breakfast is served on a sunny terrace in summer. **Map p. 112, 3B**

€€ **Locanda ai Santi Apostoli** Cannaregio 4391, Strada Nova. 041 521 2612, fax 041 521 2611, www.locandasantiapostoli.com. On the third floor of a 15th-C palace overlooking the Grand Canal, featuring antique beds, patterned damasks, and other reminders of an aristocratic past. **Map p. 124, 1B**

CASTELLO

€€ **Locanda al Leon** Castello 4270, Campo Santi Filippo e Giacomo. 041 277 0393, fax 041 521 0348, www.hotelalleon.com. Small, friendly, family-run hotel just off the Riva degli Schiavoni, a few minutes' walk from San Marco. **Map p. 146, 1B**

Metropole Castello 4149, Riva degli Schiavoni. 041 520 5044, fax 041 522 3679, www.hotelmetropole.com. Yet another prestigious address on the Riva degli Schiavoni, with stunning views over the water to San Giorgio and the Lido, delicious buffet breakfasts and a bistrot-style restaurant. **Map p. 146, 1C**

€€€ **Cipriani** Isola della Giudecca 10. 041 520 7744, fax 041 520 3930, www.hotelcipriani.it. Surely one of the world's finest hotels, also Venice's most exclusive, with luxuriously appointed rooms, a stunning garden and views that are hard to forget, its position at the tip of the Giudecca, however, makes getting into the centre rather a bother; closed Nov–Mar. **Map p. 149, 2A**

Danieli Castello 4196, Riva degli Schiavoni. 041 522 6480, fax 041 520 0208, www.starwoodhotels.com. Another of the most famous of the city's luxury hotels, where Marcel Proust stayed, breakfast is served on the roof terrace overlooking the lagoon, the island of San Giorgio and the Grand Canal. **Map p. 146, 1C**

Liassidi Palace Castello 3405, Ponte dei Greci. 041 520 5658, fax 041 522 1820, www.liassidipalacehotel.com. Newly created from a 600-year-old palace, with soaring ceilings, Gothic windows and marble floors, as well as all modern comforts and amenities. **Map p. 146, 2B**

Londra Palace Castello 4171, Riva degli Schiavoni. 041 520 0533, fax 041 522 5032, www.hotelondra.it. Near to but less ostentatious than the Danieli: still in the luxury class, it offers marvellously appointed rooms and an equally impressive roof terrace. **Map p. 146, 2C**

art glossary

Balla, Giacomo (1871–1958) Italian artist and founding member of the **Futurist** movement in painting. Two of his more significant works, *Abstract speed + sound*, 1913-14, and *Paths of movement + dynamic sequences*, 1913, are in the Peggy Guggenheim collection (see p. 68); a third, *Paths of movement + dynamic sequences*, 1913, is in the Mattioli collection at the Guggenheim museum (see p. 75).

Baroque A style in the Western arts roughly coinciding with the 17th C, though early manifestations in Italy occur in the late 16th C. Baroque painting and sculpture are distinguished by the desire to evoke emotional states by appealing to the senses, often in dramatic ways.

Bassano, Jacopo (c. 1510/18–92). Late Renaissance/early Baroque painter known for his religious paintings, lush landscapes, and scenes of everyday life. He was a pioneer of the genre scene and one of the first painters to be interested in depicting peasants: his *St Jerome the Hermit* (see p. 59) shows the saint as a member of the working class, rather than the aristocracy.

Bellini This famous family has given us three great masters of the Venetian School: Jacopo, and his sons **Gentile** and **Giovanni**. Jacopo (c. 1400–70/01) introduced the principles of Florentine early Renaissance art into Venice. The most famous surviving painting by Gentile (c. 1429/30–1507) is the large canvas of *St Mark preaching at Alexandria*, which hangs in Milan. Giovanni (1430–1516) was the leading figure of the early Renaissance in Venice. Numerous of his works show a steady evolution from purely religious, narrative emphasis to a new naturalism of setting and landscape. The *Camerlenghi Madonna* in the Accademia (see p. 56), and *Crucifixion*, *Transfiguration* and *Pietà* in the Correr, are brilliant examples of his masterful command of colour. The Correr also preserves important paintings by Jacopo.

Bellotto, Bernardo (1721–80). Nephew and pupil of **Canaletto** (see bellow). His *Scuola di San Marco at San Giovanni e Paolo* in the Accademia (see p. 60) is a masterpiece of **vedutismo**, or view painting.

Boccioni, Umberto (1882–1916) Italian painter, sculptor and theoriest of the **Futurist** movement. The Peggy Guggenheim collection (see pp. 68, 75) has one of his finest sculptures, *Dynamism of a speeding horse + houses*, 1914-15, and the Mattioli collection has three of his more celebrated paintings (see p. 75).

Canaletto, (Giovanni) Antonio (1697–1768) The most famous Venetian **vedutista** (view painter); his paintings are known for their strong contrasts of light and shade, and many were made on the spot instead of from drawings. Early masterpieces by Canaletto can be seen at Ca' Rezzonico (see p. 64).

Carpaccio, Vittore (c. 1460/65–1523/26). The greatest early Renaissance narrative painter of the Venetian school, Carpaccio trained with **Giovanni Bellini** and deeply admired **Giorgione**. His best works are the cycle of large pictures of the *Legend of St Ursula* in the Accademia (see p. 61).

Carrà, Carlo (1881–1966) One of the more influential Italian painters of the first half of the 20th C, best known for his **Futurist** and Metaphysical paintings.

Carriera, Rosalba (1675–1752) Venetian portrait painter and miniaturist, best known for her work in pastels, an originator of the Rococo style in Italy and France. There is an entire room hung with her pastel portraits at Ca' Rezzonico (see p. 66).

Chirico, Giorgio de (1880–1978) Italian painter who, with **Carlo Carrà** and **Giorgio Morandi**, founded the Pittura Metafisica movement. He is known especially for his haunting cityscapes, his figure paintings involving mannequins, and his later works in imitation of the Old Masters. His works at the Peggy Guggenheim collection (see p. 68) are examples of Pittura Metafisica.

Cima da Conegliano, Giovanni Battista (1459/60–1517/18) Venetian painter much influenced by **Giovanni Bellini** and by **Antonello da**

Messina. His works are characterized by his distinctive, atmospheric handling of volume and his bright, enamel-like palette.

Classicism and Neoclassicism Historical tradition or aesthetic attitudes based on the art of ancient Greece and Rome. Classicism refers either to the art produced in antiquity or to later art inspired by that of antiquity; Neo-Classicism always refers to the art produced later. The Italian Renaissance was the first major period to focus on Classicism. Architect Leon Battista Alberti equated Classicism with beauty: 'the harmony and concord of all the parts achieved by following well-founded rules and resulting in a unity such that nothing could be added or taken away or altered except for the worse'. In painting, artists were to choose subjects that glorified man, use figures suited to the actions being represented, and imitate the appearance of actions in the natural world.

Duchamp, Marcel (1887–1968) French artist who broke down the boundaries between works of art and everyday objects. He caused a sensation with pictures like the 1911-12 painting *Sad Young Man on a Train in the Guggenheim* (see p. 72).

Futurism (In Italian, *Futurismo*) Early 20th-C artistic movement centred in Italy that emphasized the dynamism, speed, energy, and power of the machine, and the vitality, change and restlessness of modern life.

Giorgione (c. 1477–1510) Also called Giorgio Da Castelfranco; original name Giorgio Barbarelli. This extremely influential Venetian painter who was one of the initiators of a High Renaissance style. His most famous work is the *Tempest* (c. 1505) in the Accademia (see p.56).

Gothic A style of painting, sculpture and architecture that flourished in Europe during the Middle Ages. Gothic art evolved from Romanesque art and lasted roughly from the 13th to the 15th C. Architecture was the most important and original art form during the Gothic period. The principal structural elements of Gothic architecture are ribbed vaults and pointed arches, which distribute thrust from heavy walls and ceilings in a highly efficient manner. These elements enabled Gothic masons to build much larger and taller buildings than their Romanesque predecessors and to give their structures more complicated ground plans.

The term Gothic was coined by Italian Renaissance writers who attributed the invention (and what was, to them, the non-Classical ugliness) of medieval architecture to the barbarian Goths that had destroyed the Roman Empire and its Classical culture. The term retained its derogatory overtones until the 19th C, at which time a positive critical revaluation of Gothic architecture took place.

Guardi, Francesco (1712–93) Venetian view painter whose free handling and atmospheric effects present a fascinating alternative to Canaletto's meticulous views of Venetian architecture. Most of his views of Venice were produced as souvenirs for tourists. *Fire at San Marcuola*, his masterpiece in the Accademia (see p. 60), was inspired by a real event—a fire in Venice's oil warehouses on 28 December 1789.

Humanism Although the spirit of the Renaissance ultimately took many forms, it was expressed earliest by the intellectual movement called Humanism. Humanism was initiated by secular men of letters, rather than by the scholar-clerics who had previously dominated medieval intellectual life. Its predecessors were people like Dante and Petrarch, and its chief protagonists included the Florentines Marsilio Ficino and Pico della Mirandola.

Humanism had several significant features. First, it took human nature in all of its various manifestations and achievements as its subject. Second, it stressed the unity and compatibility of the truth found in all philosophical and theological schools and systems, a doctrine known as syncretism. Third, it emphasized the dignity of man. In place of the medieval ideal of a life of penance as the highest and noblest form of human activity, the Humanists looked to the struggle of creation and the attempt to exert mastery over nature. Finally, Humanism looked forward to a rebirth of a lost human spirit and wisdom. In the course of striving to recover these lost values, however, the Humanists sparked a new spiritual and intellectual outlook and cultivated a new body of knowledge. The effect of Humanism was to help people break free from the mental strictures imposed by religious orthodoxy, to inspire free inquiry and criticism, and to inspire a new confidence in the possibilities of human thought and action.

Kandinsky, Vasily (1866–1944) Avant-garde artist born in Moscow and trained in Munich, one of the first creators of pure abstraction in modern painting. He is reprsented at the Peggy Guggenheim collection by *Landscape with Red Spots, No. 2*, 1913, and *White Cross*, 1922 (see p. 74).

Longhi, Pietro (1702–85) Venetian genre painter whose scenes of everyday patrician life in Venice are often compared with those of Hogarth. There are two important collections of his works in Venice, at Ca' Rezzonico (see p. 67) and at the Fondazione Querini Stampalia (see p. 153).

Lotto, Lorenzo (1480–1556) Late Renaissance painter known for his perceptive portraits and mystical paintings of religious subjects. He trained with **Giorgione** and **Titian** in the Venetian workshop of **Giovanni Bellini**. His *Portrait of a Gentleman in his Study*, in the Accademia (see p. 57), is one of the more enigmatic works of Renaissance portraiture.

Mannerism The style and practice that predominated in Italy from the end of the High Renaissance in the 1520s to the beginnings of the Baroque age, around 1590. Mannerism originated as a reaction to harmonious Classicism and the idealized naturalism of High Renaissance art as practiced by Leonardo and Michelangelo. In Mannerism, an obsession with style and technique in figural composition often outweighed the importance of subject matter. The highest value was placed upon the apparently effortless solution of intricate artistic problems, such as the portrayal of the nude in complex and artificial poses.

Mantegna, Andrea (1431?–1506). A painter and engraver, Andrea Mantegna was one of the foremost Italian painters of the 15th C and the first fully Renaissance artist of northern Italy. He combined the Venetian school's command of colour and composition with the interest in Classical art that reached Northern Italy from Florence. The *St Sebastian* at Ca' d'Oro (see p. 120) is one of his best-known masterpieces.

Marini, Marino (1901–1980) One of the leading Italian sculptors of the 20th C. *Angel of the City*, 1948, is probably the most famous of his horse-and-rider groups; it is conspicuously set on the Grand Canal terrace of the Peggy Guggenheim collection (see pp. 69, 75).

Miró, Joan (1893–1983) Catalan painter, lithographer, sculptor and fabric designer, one of the foremost exponents of abstract and Surrealist art. There are three works of his in the Peggy Guggenheim collection (see p. 68).

Modigliani, Amedeo (1884–1920). Painter and sculptor whose portraits and nudes are characterised by asymmetry of composition, elongation of the figure, and a simple but monumental use of line. His *Portrait of the painter Frank Haviland*, 1914, is a highlight of the Mattioli collection at Peggy Guggenheim's house (see p. 75).

Palma Vecchio (Jacopo Negretti, c. 1480–1528) Venetian painter of the High Renaissance, noted for his craftsmanship. Palma specialised in the type of contemplative religious picture known as the sacra conversazione (a group of historically unrelated sacred personages grouped together). His masterpiece is the *St Barbara* in Santa Maria Formosa (see p. 163). His grand nephew, Jacopo Palma il Giovane (1544–1628) was also a prominent painter.

Paolo Veneziano (d. ca. 1362). A leading painter in the Byzantine style in 14th-C Venice and the first great master of Venetian painting for whom we have a name; he and his two sons jointly signed the cover for the *Pala d'Oro* in St Mark's in 1345 (see p. 16). His masterpiece is the *Coronation of the Virgin* from the church of Santa Chiara, now in the Accademia (see p. 55).

Picasso, Pablo (1881–1973) Spanish expatriate painter, sculptor, printmaker, ceramicist, and stage designer, one of the most influential artists of the 20th C and the creator (with **Georges Braque**) of Cubism. The Peggy Guggenheim collection preserves fine examples of his Cubist period and two magnificent abstract paintings (see p. 71).

Pittura Metafisica School of painting that flourished mainly between 1911 and 1920 in the works of the Italian artists **Giorgio De Chirico**, **Carlo Carrà** and **Giorgio Morandi**. The artists' intention was to use representational but bizarre, incongruous imagery—juxtaposing disparate objects set into deep perspectives—to disquiet the viewer. The movement had a strong influence on the **Surrealists** in the 1920s.

Pollock, Jackson (1912–1950) Modern American painter whose career was launched in large part thanks to Peggy Guggenheim's generosity and support. A leading exponent of Abstract Expressionism, an art movement characterised by the free-associative gestures in paint sometimes referred to as 'action painting', he received widespread publicity and recognition for the radical poured, or 'drip', technique he used to create his major works. The Peggy Guggenheim collection presents a compendium of his career (see p. 74).

Renaissance Literally 'rebirth', the term Renaissance refers to the period in European civilization immediately following the Middle Ages and a surge of interest in Classical learning and values. The Renaissance originated in Florence in the early 15th C and spread throughout Italy and Europe, gradually replacing the Gothic style of the late Middle Ages. It encouraged a revival of naturalism in painting and sculpture and Classical forms and ornament in architecture

Ricci, Sebastiano (1659–1734) The first of the Venetian itinerant painters (the others were **Canaletto**, **Bellotto** and **Giambattista Tiepolo**), Ricci worked in Bologna, Rome, Modena, Florence and Parma before going to Vienna, where he worked in the Schönbrunn Palace. He also worked extensively in England.

Rococo A style of painting, architecture, sculpture and the decorative arts that originated in France in the early 18th C but was soon adopted in other countries. It is characterized by lightness, grace, elegance, and extensive use of curving, natural forms in ornamentation. The greatest Venetian master of Rococo art was Giambattista Tiepolo.

Romanesque The name Romanesque refers to the fusion of Roman, Carolingian and Ottonian, Byzantine, and Germanic traditions. It characterised European art from around 1000 to about 1150. Its geographic distribution resulted in a wide variety of local types.

Sansovino, Jacopo (Jacopo Tatti, 1486–1570) Sculptor and architect who introduced the style of the High Renaissance into Venice. He is principally famous as the designer of the Biblioteca

Marciana (see p. 33); his most famous sculptures are the gigantic *Mars and Neptune* at the head of the staircase in the Palazzo Ducale (see p. 22).

Severini, Gino (1883–1966) Painter whose synthesis of the styles of **Futurism** and **Cubism** was instrumental in gaining acceptance for the Futurist movement outside Italy. He was especially famous for his dynamic paintings of dancing figures.

Sironi, Mario (1885–1961) Italian painter and sculptor whose figural works and industrial cityscapes are among the the higher achievements of Novecento, the painting movement advocating a 'return to order' after the excesses of the early-20th-C avant gardes.

Tiepolo, Giovanni Battista (Giambattista) (1696–1770) The last of the great Venetian decorators, and arguably the greatest painter of the 18th C. Influenced by **Ricci** and **Veronese**, he is known for his luminous, poetic frescoes, with figures and architecture receding into dizzy distances beyond the picture plane (examples in Venice include four fabulous ceiling paintings at Ca' Rezzonico, see p. 66). His son Giovanni Domenico (Giandomenico, 1727–1804) was also a considerable painter in his own right, as well as his father's assistant and imitator.

Tintoretto (Jacopo Robusti, c. 1518–1594) A great Mannerist painter of the Venetian school and one of the more important artists of the late Renaissance. The brilliant cycle of paintings made for the Scuola di San Rocco in Venice is universally considered his highest achievement (see p. 95).

Titian (Tiziano Vecellio, 1488/90–1576). The greatest Renaissance painter of the Venetian school was recognized early in his own lifetime as an extraordinary painter. In 1590 the art theorist Giovanni Lomazzo declared him 'the sun amidst small stars not only among the Italians but all the painters of the world'. Titian's magnificent *Assumption of the Virgin* in the church of the Frari (see p. 91) is probably the most famous painting of the Venetian Renaissance.

Veronese, Paolo (Paolo Caliari, c. 1528–88) One of the major painters of the 16th-C Venetian school. His works usually are huge canvases depicting allegorical, biblical, or historical subjects in splendid colour. He excelled at illusionary compositions that extend the eye beyond the actual confines of the room, allowing him to introduce vast crowds of accessory figures. The licence he took with sacred subjects got him into trouble with the Inquisition. His *Marriage of St Catherine* is one of the highlights of the Accademia (see p. 58).

Verrocchio, Andrea del (1435–1488) Florentine sculptor and painter and the teacher of Leonardo da Vinci. His equestrian statue of Bartolomeo Colleoni, erected before the Scuola di San Marco in Venice in 1496, is one of the great masterpieces of the Renaissance (see p. 151).

Vivarini A family of Venetian painteers, consisting of Antonio (active 1440–1476/84), his brother Bartolommeo (active 1450–99) and Antonio's son Alvise (active 1457–1503/05). Their works show the influence of **Giovanni Bellini** and **Andrea Mantegna**.

index

art/shop/eat Venice
First edition 2005
Published by Blue Guides Limited, a Somerset Books company
The Studio, 51 Causton Street, London SWIP 4AT

ISBN 0-905131-04-6

Published in the United States of America by WW Norton & Company, Inc
500 Fifth Avenue, New York, NY 10110, USA

ISBN 0-393-32783-3

Series devised by Gemma Davies   Photo editor: Hadley Kincade
Editor: Maya Mirsky   Layout and production: Anikó Kuzmich
Consulting editor: Nigel McGilchrist Copy editing: Gemma Davies, Mark Griffith

Floorplans by Imre Bába, ©Blue Guides Limited
Maps by Dimap Bt., ©Blue Guides Limited
Printed and bound in China by SunFung Offset Binding Co.,Ltd.

Front cover: *The Parlour* by Pietro Longhi, at the Fondazione Querini
Stampalia, Venice. Bridgeman Art Library, London, www.bridgeman.co.uk
Back cover: courtesy of the Tourist Board of Venice

For permission to reproduce pictures throughout the book, grateful thanks
are due to the following: Museo Correr, Venice, Italy/Bridgeman Art Library,
London, www.bridgeman.co.uk (p. 31); La Fenice (p. 37); Ministero per i Beni e
le Attivita Culturali (pp. 59, 62-63); ©The Solomon R. Guggenheim Foundation,
New York. Photograph by David Heald ©SRGF, NY. ©ADAGP, Paris, and DACS,
London, 2004 (p. 73); Basilica Santa Maria Gloriosa dei Frari (p. 91); San
Rocco, Venice, Italy. Cameraphoto Arte Venezia, Bridgeman Art Library,
London, www.bridgeman.co.uk (p. 98); Ca' d'Oro, Venice, Italy. Bridgeman Art
Library, London, www.bridgeman.co.uk (p. 120); Salviati (p. 142); ©Damien
Hirst, Courtesy Jay Jopling/White Cube (London) (p. 170).

Photographs by Imre Baric (pp. 10, 11, 13, 16, 76, 79, 82, 85, 96, 104, 106, 110,
123, 127, 129, 139, 165, 169, 179, 187); Bill Hocker (p. 160); and Phil Robinson
(p. 33).

SOMERSET BOOKS

Mestre

Marco Polo
Airport

Torcello

Burano **p. 134**

Murano

p. 124

S. Erasmo

Venice

Le Vignole

pp. 2-3

Lido

Adriatic

Sea

Chioggia

| 0 | | 5 miles |
| 0 | | 10 kilometres |

Map

Pianta generale e avvertenze

General map and notes

Linee centrocittà

in entrambi i sensi
two ways

Linee giracittà

in senso antiorario
anticlockwise

in senso orario
clockwise

Linee lagunari

in entrambi i sensi
two ways

Linee stagionali

monodirezionali
one way

Legenda

■ 1 ■   ▬▬▬

Effettua la fermata
Does stop here

Non effettua la fermata
Does not stop here

Autobus actv	Ospedale	Ferrovia	Parcheggio	Taxi
Actv bus	*Hospital*	*Railway*	*Park*	

Avvertenze

Il passeggero deve presentarsi con il denaro contato all'acquisto del biglietto e deve controllare il biglietto e i resti in denaro all'atto della consegna.
Nessuna responsabilità può essere attribuita agli agenti addetti alla vendita se i reclami non vengono presentati tempestivamente (Ministero dei Trasporti, n.11246 del 15.10.1957 e n.4273 del 17.05.1961).

I biglietti in corso di validità non sono rimborsabili e non possono essere sostituiti.

In caso di chiusura della biglietteria il passeggero può acquistare il biglietto a bordo richiedendolo al marinaio subito dopo l'imbarco evitando così le sanzioni per mancanza di titolo di viaggio.

La mancanza del biglietto o il suo uso irregolare comporta l'applicazione delle sanzioni della Legge Regionale n.25 del 30.10.1998 che prevedono il pagamento della tariffa ordinaria più una sanzione.

Notes

Please try to prepare the right change before buying your ticket.
Important: you must check both your ticket and change as our ticket staff cannot be held responsible for complaints that are not made immediately (Ministry of Transport regulations No. 11246 of 15.10.1957 and No. 4273 of 17.05.1961).

Once you have stamped your tickrt, it cannot be refunded or replaced.

If the ticket offices are closed, you can buy your ticket on board by asking the boat attendant immediately after getting on otherwise you will have to pay a fine.

If you travel without a proper ticket or are using a ticket improperly, you will be liable for a fine (as per Regional Law No. 25 of 30.10.1998) plus the cost of the ticket.

If you have a bag, case or other item having one side longer than 50 cm, you must pay the price of a full oneway ticket.